SECRETS THE PROS WON'T TELL YOU ABOUT WINNING HOLD'EM POKER

SECRETS THE ♣
PROS WON'T TELL ♥
YOU ABOUT WINNING ♠
HOLD'EM POKER ♦

Lou Krieger and Sheree Bykofsky

LYLE STUART
Kensington Publishing Corp.
www.kensingtonbooks.com

Lou Krieger dedicates this book to the Sligo Rose, Deirdre Quinn. She is surely the best hand he's ever been dealt.

Sheree Bykofsky dedicates this book to her dear departed parents, Rosalind and Irving Bykofsky, who both played poker. She wants them to know she sees the signs that they're watching over her—especially when she wins poker tournaments.

LYLE STUART BOOKS are published by

Kensington Publishing Corp.
850 Third Avenue
New York, NY 10022

All Kensington titles, imprints, and distributed lines are available at special quantity discounts for bulk purchases for sales promotions, premiums, fund-raising, educational, or institutional use. Special book excerpts or customized printings can also be created to fit specific needs. For details, write or phone the office of the Kensington special sales manager: Kensington Publishing Corp., 850 Third Avenue, New York, NY 10022, attn: Special Sales Department; phone 1-800-221-2647.

Lyle Stuart is a trademark of Kensington Publishing Corp.

First Printing: March 2006

10 9 8 7 6 5

Printed in the United States of America

ISBN 0-8184-0659-3

Contents

v

2. Tactics, Strategies, and Ploys

3. Image   *100*

4.   Hands   *122*

5.   Money   *137*

6. Tournament Play

7. Online Play

8. Minimal Math 198

Foreword

Great teachers do not tell you *what* to think. They teach you *how* to think. There's a difference. A big difference.

At first glance, poker is such a deceptively simple game to learn. The rules take no more than a few minutes to understand, and within a relatively short time, even a beginner can be playing among seasoned veterans. No other endeavor—not competitive sports and certainly not intellectual pursuits such as chess or backgammon—gives novices the opportunity to catapult themselves into the line of fire so quickly with so little training or study. Lack of barriers is a major reason why poker is booming in popularity across the United States and abroad.

But with easy access and opportunity often comes self-deception. Many of us deceive ourselves into thinking we are good poker players, when the sad fact is that we are not. That is why poker stands alone among competitive pursuits. No other game permits rank amateurs to compete on equal footing with world-class professionals. Shooting a round of golf with Tiger Woods or playing a game of chess with a grandmaster would quickly give one a dose of reality. But sitting down at the poker table and winning a few hands—and it can happen, even if your opponents are renowned experts—can certainly be a narcotic to anyone with a bit of beginner's luck and a modicum of skill.

When it comes to trying to be objective about ourselves,

many of us simply see what we want to. Poker players are no different. We believe we can beat anybody. Sometimes we even do. And we love the game as a result.

From our very first poker experience, we develop habits and patterns of play that are often a reflection of our character and personality. Once habits are formed, it is hard to change them, and many new players who have learned their poker skills by watching the World Poker Tour or the World Series of Poker on television have learned it wrong.

Too many books and videos on the market have a paint-by-numbers approach. This is fine if you are a defending world champion or an accomplished high-limit player. But what about the bread and butter average poker player? Most players, even most good players, will benefit immensely from a bit of assistance in analyzing complex poker situations and problems in order to come up with the optimal counter strategy. To do this usually requires another pair of eyes looking over your shoulder along with some good advice you can trust. In other words, it helps to have coaches on your side who play the game well, can break down complex poker situations into easily understood problems, and clearly explain their rationale.

The two authors of this book, Lou Krieger and Sheree Bykofsky are not only great players, they are great teachers too.

The first time I met Lou Krieger, I was not a writer. I was a player, and I wrote to him. Lou wrote back and was helpful. That was followed up with a phone call. He cared; he wanted to help. He was a natural teacher. What impressed me most was his ability to break down complex strategy problems, explain them in an easy-to-understand way and retool me, the student, without ever sounding condescending.

I have not known Sheree as long as I've known Lou. But

what I know impresses me. Stealthiness is a charm in poker, and Sheree is a weapon. I think it is also great to get a woman's perspective on poker. More women are coming into poker than ever before. Whether you are a female player, or play against women, there are many insights she has—and the guys don't—that she communicates so clearly that it makes you wonder why you never saw it before.

In my twenty or so years in this business, I have been blessed to work as a player, a writer, and a casino executive. I believe I have seen the game of poker from every conceivable angle. I have seen lots of winners, and many more losers. I have been a witness to every final table at the World Series of Poker and the World Poker Open for four straight years. That's 200 of the top final tables in the world. I walk around cardrooms. I play online and in casinos almost every day. When I'm not playing poker, I'm writing about it. Poker is my life.

If you want to win the WSOP, there are many books and videos you can buy. Unfortunately, because of the nature of tournament play, none of these will make you win it. No book can guarantee that you'll win the World Series of Poker or the World Poker Open. But if you apply Lou's and Sheree's concepts to live action play, you WILL be a better poker player than you are right now. And you will have the tools to become a champion.

—Nolan Dalla
Las Vegas

Acknowledgments

Sheree's Acknowledgments

It takes a poker room! First let me thank you for reading this book. If this book helps you, please help me thank those people who helped me to help you. Foremost, Levi Rothman, whose mutterings I listened to for a year. I can still hear his words ringing in my ear, "NEVER play ace little under the gun!" and "Who is the best who ever lived?" Levi, you are one of the best who ever lived. Also, Dave Lipschutz, who always finds a way to trick me into telling him my secrets without ever revealing his—and then outmastering the master! When is your book coming out? I'd like to thank the many book authors who helped me develop my own skill set: Sklansky, Brunson, McEvoy, Caro, and of course, Krieger—but I'll get to you later.

I'd also like to thank the world-class poker players I represent as a literary agent: Gary Carson, David Apostolico, Henry Stephenson, Cat Hulbert, John Bukofsky (no relation), J. Phillip Vogel, Ephraim Rosenbaum, and even my one-time author Phil Hellmuth. (Hey, Phil, when you showed me that you folded your signature pocket nines the time I came in first and you came in second at that exhibition tournament at your publisher's, I knew you wouldn't think I was capable of bluffing, but I was. I had queen-four heads up.) Despite keeping some secrets for yourselves, your books are all great.

I'd like to thank my friends and family for their under-standing as I wrote this book, especially Ken Jacobson who took notes as I drove us to Atlantic City and proved that my strategies worked by implementing them. More friends to thank are Linda Gruber and Bob Detmer for introducing me to the game in the same serious way that we all played tournament Scrabble® together. Steve Ash, you introduced me to my favorite game ever: no-limit tournament poker. Thanks, too, to my Park Avenue poker crew whom I miss: Sam Friedman, concert pianist Abbey Simon, Jonathan Fried-man, Brian Padol, and—may he rest in peace—Ring Lard-ner, Jr. (Why did I cash that $43 check that I won from you!) Thank you Janet Rosen, my no-longer-secret agent weapon, for running the cover and working so hard as I traveled and played poker. Ed Morrow and Rita Rosen-kranz, you made our book, *Put Your House on a Diet,* a masterpiece.

I'd like to thank the poker room managers, staff, and dealers of New York City who staved off the coppers as I studied the game, played, and wrote. You know who you are! I'd even like to turn the other cheek and thank the cranky players who were sure they were losing their chips to an aggressive female who just got lucky. Thank you for paying me off! More than them, I'd like to thank the mostly lovely players in those clubs whom I truly enjoy playing with. And from the Trop to the Mirage, I love the legal poker rooms I play in, too—especially the Taj Mahal, where Tom Gitto runs my favorite poker room, and where the hidden poker snack bar serves the best food in Atlantic City (secret #1). A million thanks for hosting our first *Poker Life* Poker Author Tournament.

I'd like to thank Poker Stars for providing a great site that allowed me to live one of my dreams of playing in the World Series of Poker. And thanks to the many people who were pulling for me, including Marty Edelston and the other wonderful people at Boardroom Reports.

Pocket aces to everyone at Kensington, especially my friend and editor Richard Ember, one of the nicest editors in publishing, Kristen Hayes, who was responsible for the brilliant book cover, and Bob Shuman, a most excellent copyeditor.

Mostly, I would like to thank Lou Krieger whose friendship, talent, knowledge and professionalism made writing this book one of the best experiences of my whole life. Lou, you are the greatest!

Lou's Acknowedgments

My dad got me started playing poker. I was seven or eight years old and once a week he hosted a game around the kitchen table in our working class Brooklyn neighborhood. I badgered my mother for weeks to let me stay up and watch them play, until she finally relented. I was sweating the game, and all the men from the neighborhood who played were kind enough to explain the rules to me. After a while I understood what was going on and when I knew, I was hooked.

Poker was cool, and I loved it. I only had two restrictions: never allow my actions to give away anyone's hand, and never repeat the more colorful phrases I heard at the table in front of my mother. Most of the Yiddish and Sicilian epithets I know today, I learned at the poker table as an eight-year-old.

Poker seemed like some sort of secret adults' club, and I was accepted. After all, what eight-year-old kid doesn't want to feel like an adult and an insider too?

That was the tipping point, although I didn't realize it at the time and never grew up intending to play poker and write about it. But the seeds were sewn and I want to thank my father, who died way too young, for pointing me in this direction—though neither of us knew it then. I want to thank my mom, too. She lived a long, full life and always trusted her sons to do the right thing, even when it involved all-night poker games and the kinds of insane deadlines writers learn to live with.

I've met some of the most interesting people in my life through poker, and all of them have been encouraging. Al Alvarez, author of *The Biggest Game in Town*, and a major figure in contemporary literature, was kind enough to encourage me over dinner at the Victoria Club in London when I was immersed in my first book and filled with doubt. I'm sure he has no idea how helpful his advice was, but I'd like to thank him for helping me *get over* with my first book. The seven others that followed over the next few years leave a trail that harkens back to his kind words about my writing.

There are other poker writers I admire, and they've all become friends as well as colleagues. This group includes: Dave Scharf, Amy Calistri, Barbara Connors, Pauly McGuire, Ashley Adams, and Kathy Watterson. I also want to thank Mickey Wilson at PokerMagazine.com for providing an online outlet for my writing.

I want to thank everyone who attends BARGE, poker's annual gathering of players who form friendships online and continue them in person every year. You are surely poker's brightest and best.

Thanks, also, to the folks at Royal Vegas Poker for their continuing support and encouragement. I also want to thank Ron and Amber Oberman, Paul and Kimyo Zibits, Linda Johnson, Jan Fisher, and Mark and Lisa Tenner. Thanks, too, to all the guys and gals at the home game in Orange County that I almost never attend since I moved to Palm Desert but see periodically anyway.

Thank you to long-time friends Dan and Sharon Goldman, Nolan and Marietta Dalla, and to the gang that plays online every Wednesday night in Royal Vegas Poker's "Play the Experts" tournament: Max Shapiro, Barbara Enright, Dr. Al Schoonmaker, Mike Cappelletti, Matt Lessinger, and Rose Richie.

I also want to thank Rick and Barbara, Stan and Phyllis, Marv and Joyce, Mike and Marci, Lenny and Susan, Alan and Myrna, George and Fran, George and Rita and a few others with whom I've kept in touch since elementary school and high school. It's been a terrific lifetime of memories.

I also want to thank my co-author, Sheree Bykofsky, who is a wonderful writer and a terrific agent, too. Thanks to everyone at Kensington—though I know you only through e-mail—you did a grand job in getting this book together. Your suggestions were terrific, the editing made things much more readable, and the cover is as bright and attractive as the contents.

I began these acknowledgments with family, and I'll end with family, too. Thanks to David, Karen, and Abby, and to Philip, Freda, Quinn, and Michael; Shannon and Shandie; and Heather, Scott, and Shelby too. Special thanks and acknowledgment to my wife, Deirdre Quinn, who managed to make her way from Sligo, Ireland, to Montana, then Washington, and finally to Palm Desert. It was there she learned that hot climates are better than cold ones, and how to nurture a moderately compulsive writer, poker player, and husband.

Introduction

There's a feeding frenzy going on. In the 2003 World Series of Poker, the improbably named Chris Moneymaker took $2,500,000 after winning his $10,000 buy-in at a $40 satellite on the Internet. This scenario was repeated in 2004, when nearly 2,600 players ponied up $10,000 to enter the World Series of Poker's main event. Greg Raymer, who won his buy-in online, came away with the winner's share of $5,000,000. In 2005, every player at the final table became an instant millionaire. The winner, Joseph Hachem, took away a record-breaking $7,500,000.

Repeat showings of the World Series of Poker on ESPN, along with the World Poker Tour on the Travel Channel and England's *Late Night Poker*, have supercharged a worldwide interest in the game. These TV shows found higher viewership in reruns than they did during original showings, which is something that almost never happens in the world of TV. It points to an unflagging interest in poker.

This has resulted in a publishing bonanza for poker books. Although almost every one of them is an instructional book, they provide new players with enough strategy and tactics to survive, and maybe even win, in recreational poker games. Most of these books elucidate the game at its most basic level: how to play; what beats what; which hand to start, raise or fold with. We know all about these books;

author Lou Krieger wrote seven best-selling poker instructionals himself.

You can read scads of instructional books on poker and not even realize that most authors—many of whom are expert players—have withheld their best secrets. This allows the authors to teach poker basics while retaining enough private knowledge to beat *you* the next time they sit down at your table.

Are you curious about the secrets of winning hold'em poker that no pro will tell you in a how-to book? The multiple layers of the game only reveal themselves over time after much study, patience, experience, and deliberation. We intend to reveal as many of these secrets as possible in *Secrets the Pros Won't Tell You About Winning Hold'em Poker*. Poker is a game of skill rather than luck; and there are many tools you can use to beat another player. We will tell you the best ways to counter plays by both good and bad players. We aim to show you the art of Texas hold'em poker—to help you get a more accurate *feel* for the game.

Because poker is a game of skill, serious players are always looking for an edge. And competition is tough. The newer breed of poker player, those weaned on Internet poker sites and games in college dorms, are a studious breed. They're readers, computer literate, and, like former world champion Chris Ferguson, many of them spend a significant amount of time testing poker theories on a PC—quite a departure from the old, back-room image of a cigar-chewing gambler who never read anything that wasn't found in the racing form.

Our aim here is to turn you into a professional-level player. We also want you to enjoy an easy and fun read. It is far better to absorb complex strategies than to memorize them. Therefore, each of the concepts and playing strategies in this book will be discussed and organized as part of a few broad themes: basic concepts and play; tactics, strategies and ploys; image; money; minimal math; tournament play; playing; and growing as a player. But please note that poker is extremely addictive and potentially dangerous in many ways. We encourage anyone who gambles to do so responsibly.

Here's a bonus secret to start you off:

Two Books in One

This book is really two books in one. It's filled with secrets that you can use yourself. It's also filled with information about what other people—particularly experts—do. Knowing how the pros are playing will help you win! We know, for example, when a tournament player has just read Doyle Brunson's *Super System*. The player is super-aggressive. He'll go all out and make large aggressive bets against weak or timid players at every opportunity. If you're in a gambling mood, raise or reraise this player more often!

Now, let's begin!

Note: Just like poker players, human language is flawed—in its extensive use of the masculine pronoun. And just as good poker players mix up their hands, we've mixed up our use of male and female pronouns throughout the text—roughly in proportion to the ratio of men and women who play serious poker today. Although, as coauthor Sheree Bykofsky exemplifies, more and more women are becoming true players, the game of poker is still largely part of the domain of men.

1

BASIC CONCEPTS AND PLAY

Gestalt n. A configuration or pattern of elements so unified as a whole that it cannot be described merely as a sum of its parts.

—WordNet 1.7

This section comprises a compendium of poker tips that span the spectrum of poker sophistication. Some tips may cover familiar ground while others may explain new thought processes.

If you're looking for basic hold'em elements, such as the ranking of hands and suggested starting card combinations, you won't find them here. In this section you'll find concepts and tips that are *basic and essential to professional poker players*—guys and gals who earn either all or a significant part of their livings at the poker table. When you allow these concepts to bake like a cake in your mind, as they do, you'll find yourself inventing new secrets for yourself each and every time you play.

Extrasensory Perception

It is a euphoric feeling when the beginner realizes that although each player is dealt two personal, private cards, it is sometimes possible to know with near certainty what someone's two hidden cards are. It's almost as though you can see through both the cards and a player's skull to gather the information that you need to make a good call, a good fold, or a great bluff. This doesn't happen all the time, however, and none of this is 100 percent certain. If it were, poker wouldn't be much of a game. But the necessity to act on incomplete information is what makes poker as richly textured as it is.

And *incomplete* can be all over the lot. Even expert players experience hands where they're flying blind and have no idea what in the world an opponent may be holding. Yet there are other moments of insight, usually derived from knowing a particular opponent's playing proclivities. One must watch patterns: Is he aggressive, raising at every opportunity, or is he quietly calling? Such information will reveal the cards to you just as surely as if he were playing with his hand face up. Sometimes moments of insight just seem to spring fully blown into one's consciousness. Far more often it is the result of deductive reasoning combined with the knowledge of an opponent's playing style, and this analytical process can be learned.

Assessing New Games

If you are the new player at an established game and you see that everyone folds when one player bets, be careful when calling him. He probably only raises with premium hands. Similarly, if one player raises and everyone else calls, it's probable that this player raises with less-than-premium hands. It's important to spend some time checking over the game you're playing in when you first sit down. In fact, if you have a good vantage point, you should be clocking the game even before you are seated at the table. Fifteen to twenty minutes should be time enough to get a good handle on your opponents. Here's what to look for:

- Happy games, lots of chips, a jovial table atmosphere. This typifies a game full of players who are having fun. Players enjoying themselves tend to be a lot looser than those who are scrutinizing everything that goes on. If you see lots of friendly flirting going on, that's good, too. And if your opponents are drinking anything stronger than bottled water, that's also a good sign.
- Who's loose, who's tight? Within a few minutes you should have a handle on which players are callers, which are aggressive, and who won't gamble unless they have unbeatable hands. There are all sorts of clues to loose play in addition to the obvious ones, such as seeing the kinds of hands they show down. This is a clue to the kinds of starting hands they're prone to play in early, middle, or late position.
- Who's passive, who's aggressive? You can be loose and passive as well as loose and aggressive. You can be tight and passive as well as tight and aggressive. Obviously, the aggressive profiles are more dangerous because they are less likely to get out of your way when you bet, might not throw away a hand if you bluff, and may even play back at you by reraising with or without a strong hand.

- Watch every showdown. Look closely whenever a hand is turned face up at its conclusion. Then replay the hand in your mind. Try to scope out the players in that pot based on how they bet and reacted to bets and raises, given the hands that they were holding. This is the absolute best way to learn the playing styles of your opponents.

- Who's winning, who's losing? While winners tend to be the better players, the short-term variance in poker can play havoc with judgment when all you have is fifteen minutes to determine which players seem to be doing well and which ones are stuck for the day. Chip stacks aren't always good indicators. Some players just buy in for more money than others. And, although twenty-five big bets is a typical buy-in ($1,000 in a $20–$40 game), some players will buy in for $1,500 to $2,000. Others will sit down with between $500 and $800 in front of them. But if you examine chip stacks and correlate them with a person's demeanor—happy or sad, upbeat or morose, outgoing or introspective—you should have a good idea about the game's winners and losers.

- It matters where you sit relative to aggressive, good players, and their chips. In an ideal world, you want the tough, aggressive players on your right along with any maniacs at the table. This is so you can get out of the way of the good players, unless you have a very strong hand. Raise the maniac with any reasonable hand, so that you can play heads up against him. You want the tight, cautious, conservative players on your left, so you can bet them out of the pot. They don't represent all that much of a threat to you since they tend to raise infrequently, if at all.

If you happen to have an aggressive player on your left, you have to constrain the number of hands you play. When you have a good hand, though, you can let your aggressive tablemate do your betting for you; you may be able to trap him for a lot of chips by hand's end.

Any time you have someone's number, you should try to sit to his left. This is especially true if he has a big stack because the money flows left. Poker expert Mike Caro first pointed out that money flows clockwise around a table. If you could sit on the ceiling and watch the game, you'd see a time-lapse photography swirl as the money moves in that direction. So, if you can sit to the left of a player with a big stack of money, count your blessings; some of it figures to be yours.

If you do find a maniac on your left or a player with a huge stack, think about making the money on the table flow backward to you and reraise with your good hands. This usually results in you playing the pot heads up with the maniac (who presumably raised with a lesser hand than yours). That makes you the favorite. He'll win his share of pots, but you'll win your share, too. Since you are entering pots with cards that figure to be superior to his, you'll come away the winner more often.

A Maniac on the Loose

Let's describe the characteristics of a typical maniac. If you bet, he'll raise—even when he doesn't have a hand to support his action. If you check, he'll bet. He, on the other hand, seldom checks, unless he is in early position, really has the goods, and is trying to trap a number of opponents by check-raising.

When someone bets, the maniac usually raises. If you reraise, he is more likely to make it four bets than give you credit for a big hand and simply call. He personifies an action player—albeit one who consistently shows too much speed by deliberately overvaluing and overplaying his hand. He wants to get as much money in the pot as often as possible, and frequently he does. Maniacs are ego driven. Betting, raising, or reraising is the measure of a maniac's manhood; he'd rather bully you out of a pot than beat you in a showdown. Maniacs also self-destruct and go broke quite regularly, but not before taking a number of other players down with them.

With a maniac at your table, you need to be aware of the changes his presence invariably brings. Because of his propensity for raising and reraising, more of your chips will be at risk. Lose, and you're likely to lose more than you otherwise would. Wins are also likely to be bigger. If you are a winning player, a maniac in your game will usually increase your average winnings in the long run. While it is likely to be a measurable increase, however, it probably won't be off the charts. On the other hand, there will be a dramatic increase in the fluctuations you can expect on an hourly basis. In the short run, you are susceptible to large swings, since you'll be putting more chips at risk almost every time you play a hand. If you are on a limited bankroll, or have a hard time adapting to this kind of volatility, you might want to avoid games with maniacs in them.

Don't Get Involved in a New Game Too Soon

It takes a good fifteen minutes or so to get the lay of the land. Sure, if you're dealt a big pocket pair, like aces or kings, you can get involved in a pot. You'll figure to come away with the money at the end of the hand. But stay away from speculative hands until you've got your opponents characterized and know their playing propensities. A good rule of thumb is to try to win the first hand you play to conclusion. If you do that, you will have established yourself as a good, tough player in the mind of your adversaries, and you'll be off to a great start. And by trying to win the first hand you play, you are saying, in essence, that you will avoid all but the very best hands when you first sit down at the table.

Seat Selection Is Critical Against Aggressive Players

Seat selection is critical when playing against a maniac. Always position yourself to his left. Since the maniac will raise on weak hands, as well as his better ones, you want to be in position to reraise whenever you have a strong hand. Whenever you are able to make it three bets before the flop, you stand a good chance of playing heads up against the maniac. Since you will usually be reraising on hands that are significantly stronger than his, you'll hold the advantage throughout the play of the hand.

In addition, other opponents may recognize that you're a very aggressive, though highly selective player. Your actions will demonstrate that you have no fear of the maniac. Although your opponents will seldom admit it, many of them are apprehensive whenever a maniac joins a game. Since you will only reraise before the flop with hands that have some intrinsic value, other opponents will respect your raises—regardless of whether or not the maniac is active in the hand. This, of course, provides excellent support for an occasional bluff, particularly on those occasions when you're involved in a hand with fairly tight, weak, or timid players. Remember, they've watched you slug it out with the maniac, and show down a real hand whenever you're called.

While maniacs can raise your stress level and blood pressure, remember this: They're ultimately no stronger than the cards they hold. Frequently, they're a lot weaker. As long as you position yourself to act after the maniac, and can withstand the highly volatile nature of the game, you'll be favored in the long run. After all, a maniac's worst enemy is himself. They're aggressive all right, but seldom selective. They know one tune, and one tune only—although they play it incessantly, wielding it over their opponents like a whip. Their only strength is also their greatest weakness, and when you learn to deflect their one-note strategy and use it to your advantage, the crack of their own whip can also destroy them.

Develop a Theory

Develop a theory about everyone at the table as soon as possible. Pay attention and revise accordingly. Here are some valuable observations you might make that can put money in your pocket. Watch the player who:

> Overvalues his cards
> Can't miss a flop
> Won't fold if he has good cards—even if it misses the flop
> Is a nonbeliever. Always thinks everyone is bluffing
> Bluffs too much
> Plays too many hands

Never bluffs
Is tricky
Never misses a chance to check-raise
Is too aggressive
Is too tight
Is too loose

Starting Hands Change Value in Very Aggressive Games

Starting hands change in value when there's a maniac playing. When you figure to be raised, you can't play hands like 9♦8♠. Suited connectors do best in unraised, multiway pots, when you're trying to get in cheaply. You're hoping that you'll flop a big hand against a relatively large number of opponents—who, presumably, will pay you off if you're lucky enough to flop a big hand that holds up. The only time you can play smaller, suited connectors against a maniac is from late position. In this case, the maniac has already acted and hasn't raised, and you figure you have a good chance to see the flop for one bet against a relatively large number of opponents.

You'll find yourself passing on a lot of hands you'd usually play in a less frenetic game, and it can be frustrating. Nevertheless, you don't want to commit two bets on hands that are long shots—particularly when the fear of a raise from the maniac will constrict the number of opponents you'd otherwise expect.

Why Reraising Can Be Mandatory, Not Discretionary, in Aggressive Games

Pairs and big cards go up in value. If you're holding 9-9, and the maniac raises before you act, you *must* reraise in order to constrict the number of opponents you'll play against. If you're lucky, you'll find yourself heads up with the maniac. When you're heads up against an opponent who raises on anything—or nothing—you are favored when you hold a pair. Sure, there'll be times when the maniac really has a big hand, but there'll be many more times when you'll find that he raised with absolutely nothing. That's when you'll capture the pot.

If you hold a hand like A-K or A-Q, you can also reraise and try to get heads up against the maniac. If you flop a pair, you figure to have the best hand. That's not the problem. The problem is what happens when the flop is three rags. If you're holding A-Q and the flop is 8-6-3, what should you do when the maniac bets? Since he frequently raises on anything, he's just as likely to have caught a pair—or even flopped a set—than he is to have missed the flop entirely with a hand like J-9.

You can't be certain. Since the maniac may well reraise if you try to define your own hand by raising, you're in a guessing situation. These are hands where you might decide to *gamble* with him. You might also employ a strategy of sometimes releasing your hand when the flop doesn't fit and sometimes hanging in there—so he knows he can't run you off the pot every time you raise and catch a ragged flop. It's a judgment call—and not an easy one at that. Sometimes you have to call or bluff-raise—even though you are an underdog to capture the pot. Do this simply because you are giving up too much of an edge if you allow him to bet and take the pot every time you're heads up and the flop is unfavorable to you.

If you're lucky, you'll catch enough flops with your bigger hands. You'll be able to check and call on the flop and try for a check-raise on the turn or river. This might slow down the maniac a bit since he'll eventually learn that a check on your part doesn't always imply weakness. There are, however, many maniacs who just ignore these subtler features of the game. They prefer to wield a bludgeon rather than a rapier. When you're playing against a maniac of this magnitude, forget all about subtlety. It won't work. You'll need to make some big hands, have him do your betting for you, and build the pot—which, of course, he'll gladly do—and then snap him off with a check-raise that he'll invariably call.

The Playing Zone

The concept of a *playing zone* is one that's frequently alluded to by poker theorists. You most often hear about it, in analyses regarding how specific hands were played, rather than in a broader, more conceptual context.

When one thinks of a playing zone in poker, it's usually in regard to flop games such as Texas hold'em, Omaha/8, or Omaha high-only, rather than board games, like 7-card stud or razz. Visualizing a playing zone facilitates decision-making during a hand—as well as during post mortem analyses of hands already played. It helps focus in on what cards are likely to help opponents while understanding that others might not help them at all.

Sometimes Even Hands Like Top Pair/Top Kicker Are Vulnerable . . .

Here's an example. Suppose you're playing $20–$40 hold'em and have been dealt A-Q in the big blind. Someone raises and you call, along with a few other players. The flop is Q-J-T and, for the sake of this example, we'll assume that the suits are irrelevant and that the possibilities of a flush are nonexistent. With your cards and this flop, how do you like your hand? The upside is that you've flopped top pair with top kicker, and that combination wins plenty of hold'em confrontations. But there's a dark cloud gathering, too. The three cards that flopped were all in the playing zone—that area where many other active players are likely to have holdings.

With a sequenced flop of high cards coming on the heels of a raise, it's entirely possible that your top-pair, top-kicker combination is already a big underdog. Even if you're not losing the race right now, there are rafts of turn cards that can kill you. The raiser is far ahead of you if he's holding pocket aces, pocket kings, or A-K. He also could have raised with pocket queens, jacks, or tens, and flopped a set. Even if he raised with a modest pair of nines, he's got a few outs to beat you. And if anyone called the initial raise with a hand like Q-J or J-T, they're ahead of you too.

You'd love to see a king jump out of the deck on the turn, since it's the only perfectly safe card you can catch. But it has a downside too. Anyone with as little as a naked ace would chop the pot with you. An ace on the turn gives you two pair, but it kills you if any of your opponents were in the hand with a pair of kings or a hand like K-10. Even a queen would be a mixed blessing—the trip queens you'd make might already be bested if any of your adversaries had flopped a straight or a set. You're in trouble, dude. It's about as bad as things could be, considering that you flopped the usually joy-provoking top pair, top kicker.

. . . Sometimes They Look Downright Unbeatable

But let's look at a somewhat different set of circumstances. All the players are the same and you're still holding A-Q. This time the flop is Q-7-2 and once again we'll assume that suits are irrelevant. Now top pair, top kicker looks a lot sweeter. You're still running behind the pre-flop raiser. If he has a pair of aces or kings, you're not at all in jeopardy to much else. Anyone who called the raise before the flop with a smaller pair than queens—or with connectors like A-K, K-Q, Q-J, J-10, or other generally playable hands—is an underdog and likely to throw their hand away, leaving you and the preflop raiser to duel it out heads-up.

Sure, you could be skewered if someone was playing Q-7, Q-2, or even 7-2, but most sane players are going to avoid those hands in a $20–$40 game. Your only real danger is if one of your opponents flopped a set of sevens or deuces. However, by the time you arrive at the conclusion that he might have three-of-a-kind, it will have cost you some chips and there's really not much that can be done about it. Whenever an opponent flops a set to a safe looking board, it will cost you some chips before you realize just how good a hand he might be holding. Still, this scenario is a lot safer for you than the previous one because the board was not coordinated, and two of the three cards that flopped were far outside of the playing zone.

An Accordion-Style Playing Zone

Poker is never as simple as it first appears. Suppose you were in a loose, passive, low-limit hold'em game—where seven or eight players routinely see the flop. In a game like this, the playing zone is very different. In fact, in a game that's loose enough, the playing zone often embraces the entire deck. Players are liable to turn up with any kind of hand. Losing to an opponent who runs down your A-Q with a hand like Q-2—because he was fortunate enough to catch one of three remaining deuces on the river—might be exasperating, but it's not all that uncommon.

With an extended playing zone that's stretched out like

an accordion, you can't take too much for granted. A hand like top pair, top kicker can be very vulnerable simply because any card that doesn't directly help you might help another player. The playing zone's width goes directly to a hand selection and playing strategy. In a loose, passive game with seven or eight players staying to see the flop, holdings like A-x suited gain in value because they can improve to very big hands. Others—the kind that figure to leave you with top pair, big kicker when you catch part of the flop—can be as vulnerable as they are valuable in games with much narrower playing zones.

In loose, lower-limit games, an ace on the board frequently extends the playing zone dramatically. It's a pretty rare day when an opponent is holding a hand like K-3 and makes two pair because a trey jumps out of the deck on the river. But since many players in these games are prone to play any ace they are dealt, you're never too sure which cards are safe. While it's more likely that a board with an ace and all big cards is likely to give another player two pair, even unsequenced lower cards can help someone. This is particularly true when the majority of players take the flop. Any one of them who catches any part of it is likely to stick around for the duration. You can lose a chunk of change in these games with hands like A-K. You flop top pair with the best possible kicker and the board looks like it didn't help a soul. But wait. In loose, lower-limit games, the board might just help someone simply because he or she is prone to play any ace at all.

Omaha Playing Zone

In Omaha, the playing zone—or zones; there are really two of them in Omaha/8—concept is equally important. Perhaps it's even more so, because with six two-card combinations that can be made from the four cards in your hand, a lot of probable hands become possible. For example, if you've been dealt A-2-K-K in an Omaha/8 game and the flop is K-3-8 of mixed suits, two playing zones have been touched. The two low cards that flopped mean anyone with a low draw that hasn't been counterfeited will stick around to the river trying to capture half of the pot. You don't have any worries at this juncture about a straight draw panning out, so your set of kings is currently in the lead. But sets are not the powerhouse in Omaha/8 that they are in Texas hold'em. Even if they hold up, you might wind up with only half the pot instead of the whole enchilada. Nevertheless, you are drawing to the nut low, so even if another player also holds an A-2, you'll get half of the low end of the pot as long as a third low card doesn't duplicate the ace or deuce in your hand. And even if you don't improve your set, those trip kings may hold up for the high end of the pot.

Two Playing Zones in Split-Pot Games

In Omaha/8 and other split-pot games, the playing zones lie at the deck's polar extremes. You'd like to jump into the fray with a handful of big cards, a handful of babies, or some combination like A-2-3-K. This gives you big and little coordinated combinations—and if your ace and king are suited to one or both of the babies, so much the better. The vast mid-range of the deck is not where the playing zone is located at all. While you could make a straight, if you begin with hands like 9-8-7-6, someone else is likely to make a low hand. Yet another player could make a bigger straight and you'd find yourself doomed in both directions.

But in an Omaha high-only game, a run of four mid-range cards like 9-8-7-6 works because the playing zone extends down to the middle of the deck. Although mid-range cards are dogs in Omaha/8, they are part of the playing zone for Omaha high-only. Low cards, which are death in Omaha high-only, can be raising hands in Omaha/8.

When you're playing poker, always look to the playing zone when attempting to determine what kind of hands other players might be holding, or when you're trying to make an assessment of how safe or vulnerable your own hand might be. Always remember that the playing zone is neither fixed nor immutable. It changes depending on the game and your opponents. Sane players play sane hands, and you can often determine where you stand in relation to them by understanding the playing zone and how your hand and your opponents' probable holdings relate to it. But in loose games—the kind where everyone sticks around to see the flop—the playing zone is unbounded and might even extend across the entire deck. When you're in a game like that, be careful. When it's tough to put your opponent on a hand, it's difficult to know how your hand stacks up against his.

It's times like these when you're likely to find yourself losing pots you figured you'd win. But the silver lining in this cloud of increased fluctuations and variance is that all of those excess callers make for bigger pots when you win them. And winning money is what poker is all about.

You Can Beat Bad Players and You Can Bluff Good Players

Weak players make two mistakes above all others. First, they call too often. Second, they don't fold often enough. Most recreational players are eager to play poker when they visit a card room. They don't venture out to the casino in anticipation of folding hand after hand. Playing too many hands generally involves starting out with cards that probably shouldn't be played. That error is compounded when players stick around with long-shot draws that have no chance of winning. These players have come to play, and they sleep very well, thank you, knowing that no one is going to bluff them out of a pot.

But that's not what good poker is all about. Playing poker to win can be boring because most of the time you'll be dealt a hand you really don't want to, or shouldn't, play. Good play involves throwing most of the hands you're dealt face down in the muck. All of the good players do that most of the time. On those occasions when they don't, there are two important conditions. Are they in a short-handed game where more risk-taking is required and more hands must be played? Are they at a table full of passive players who seldom bluff and raise infrequently? With this kind of texture, the pro knows he can play more speculative hands with little chance of being raised. He can either complete a big hand with assurance that his opponents will call him all the way to the bitter end, or he can release his hand at the first sign that an opponent has a better hand than he does. He'll deviate from this pattern of play only rarely, and usually when he is confronting a passive opponent who is willing to throw even good-but-not great hands away in the face of a bet or a raise. When the pro is facing this kind of opponent, the cards he holds have no meaning whatsoever. The only thing that does matter is how often he can bet or raise with a reasonable assurance that his adversary will release his hand in the face of un-mitigated aggression.

Most opponents call too much and stay in the pot far too long with weak hands. They can be beaten by betting for value, not by bluffing. Most of the time, when you bet, they're going to call. Therefore, don't bluff, but bet when you think you have the best of it, secure in the knowledge that your opponent is very likely to call you with a lesser hand.

Better Players Fold More Frequently

Good players fold all the time. They fold if they have the worst of it, and they'll also fold to a good bluff made by a solid player who bets when the cards suggest he actually has a big hand, even when he doesn't. That's not to say a good player is going to fold every time you bet into him. Sometimes he'll have a good hand and call, or a better hand and then he'll raise. Sometimes he might read you for a bluff. He'll raise just to steal the momentum and cause you to fold a weak hand. But good players can be bluffed, and that's because they are both selective and aggressive. The selectivity quotient in their game dictates that they fold some hands because they're looking for better spots to risk their money.

This is where the art of poker comes into play, and it's an art that begins with knowing one's opponent. Some can be bluffed while others will never fold if there's even the slightest inkling that they have the best hand. So, it's clear that what works against one opponent might not work against another.

Bad Beats Can Be Your Best Friends

No one's happy to see a pocket pair of aces run down at the river by someone who called your raise with a measly 6-4 offsuit. That player was very lucky when his two pair held up and beat you out of a big pot. It's no fun, either, when you flop a set and lose to two running cards that give an opponent a flush or a straight. This is particularly true when your opponent lacks any understanding of odds and outs and should not have been in the pot with you.

Still, there is a nice, shiny, silver lining to bad beats. A bad beat is the handwriting on the wall telling you that there are others in the game who play horribly. They are continuing to call your bets against all odds—or, at least, against most of the odds. You'll remember when they catch two- and three-outers to beat you. But you don't even realize it when they call the flop, call the turn, and maybe even call a bet on the river, too, only to muck their pathetic holdings when you show yours down. They couldn't beat the hand you started with and never even caught up. And you know what? They'll do that a lot more often than they'll run you down.

If you never had a bad beat, that would be a sign that you're playing in a game with really skilled players. They know all the odds and outs and don't take risks unless their investment is offset by a positive, long-term expectation. Expert players might be terrific to include in your poker discussion group because you'll probably learn a lot from them, but they are not really the ones you want to play against on a daily basis. When you play poker, you hope to find a table with a few players who always take the worst of it with long odds, get lucky just enough to ensure they keep coming back for more, and continue to contribute to your bankroll and success as a poker player.

Chip Entitlement

Many pros won't tell you that no one is entitled to your chips. They won't tell you that because so many pros do feel entitled to your chips. If you're better than they think, you can use this information to hurt them and to help yourself.

If someone sitting to your left cold calls, that is, puts in two bets without ever having put in one bet every time you raise, or if he limps whenever you limp, or raises whenever you limp, he probably has you targeted as a poor player. He thinks he'll win your chips. If he is clearly working hard to isolate you, you must make it your business to tighten up your starting hands and strategize ways to trap him before he knows that you're on to him. If you surreptitiously study him, you'll know when he's going to bet or raise. You can then seize every opportunity to maximize the number of bets that he is going to place into the pots. If you've got him beat, be especially sure to bet the river. You can't give one free card to the player who failed to respect you.

Bad Calls

It's very profitable to notice which players make bad calls. Whether you raise or someone else raises, is there a player who always calls? Bingo, you've found him. He can't always have a good calling hand. See how often he takes down the pot when he has called someone else's raise. What does he do when he has a good hand?

Call the Rocks and You're on the Rocks

There are some people you should never call when they raise. It's good to *be* that person. But you don't want to be too tight. If you do, you'll be leaving money on the table that you could have won with some of the hands you probably folded. Too tight is no good and neither is too loose. If you never lose the hands you play, you are certainly playing too tightly. So let that be your guide.

One Bluffer to a Hand

There usually aren't two bluffers at the river. If one player bets, anyone else who either calls or raises can be counted on to have a legitimate hand. Sometimes you'll find players who will bluff-raise, but it happens infrequently.

Respect

Everyone deserves respect. Even the worst player can teach you something. You will not get the respect you occasionally require if you respect no one at the table. It's an unwritten law of poker. Poker is the great equalizer, and it's the cards that do the equalizing. Poker is not a boxing match where the better fighter can impose his will on the lesser. Every time a new card comes off the deck, the relative strength of the combatants can change.

Gap Concept

If the game is pot-limit, no-limit, and especially in a no-limit tournament, the chances of succeeding are even better. Because of the size of the bets, and the fact that one misstep in a tournament can put you on the rail, players need a much bigger hand to call a raise than to do the raising. The gap between hands that are worth betting or raising and those that can call a bet or a raise, provide fertile ground for bluff bets and raises. Every top tournament player knows about "the gap," as poker expert David Sklansky has called it, and top professionals use it to exploit less skilled players at every opportunity.

Domination

One of the recurring issues discussed on Internet poker forums, and by players who belong to poker study groups, deals with the concept of dominated hands. Entire books on poker strategy have been written on the concept. Here's how it works: If I'm holding A-10, and you have A-K, my hand is *dominated*. Miraculous straights and flushes that might accrue to A-10 notwithstanding, I have three outs and three outs only to win this pot. And while there are a few more hands that will enable me to split the pot—a rainbow coalition of K-Q-J-10 might hit the board and our straights will propel us to a split pot—that's beside the point. My objective is to win, not play a lesser hand in hopes of getting my money back courtesy of a really miraculous fall of cards.

Dominated Hands Are Big Long Shots

Dominated hands, by definition, have three outs. Except for those aforementioned miraculous straights and flushes, and a few oddball split pots, only three cards will enable a dominated hand to win the pot. The hand that's doing the dominating owns the rest of the deck!

Regardless of whether opponents seem to make three-outers with regularity, no poker player wants a foot on his throat with only three cards enabling escape. Sometimes it's not even as good as all that. If the dominating hand is fortunate enough to make two pair, then for all intents and purposes you're drawing dead. Imagine that. You pair your kicker on the turn or river and bet, or even raise, thinking yours is the best hand. But your hand is still dominated; and what's worse is that your two pair will probably result in a bigger loss. This is especially true if you are frisky and do some raising with what you think is best hand; but the truth is that you are dominated and made crying calls all the way to the river.

Dominated hands are trouble. And when you've got

trouble it's time to ask yourself, "What can I do about it?" and "How can I avoid getting in situations like this in the first place?"

Trouble Hands Are Frequently Dominated

Many poker authors who write about Texas hold'em have gone to great lengths to discuss what they euphemistically call *trouble hands*. After all, lots of hands fall into this category. In early position, hands like A-J, A-10, K-J, K-10 and Q-J are classic trouble hands. "Call with hands like these in an early position," you're invariably admonished, "and you're in big trouble if an opponent raises." After all, conventional wisdom holds that most of your opponents will raise most of the time with hands that are better than those. The person doing the raising is much more likely to have a hand like A-A, K-K, A-K, or A-Q than a trouble hand. That's the "book" move.

While that's true as far as it goes, the fact remains that many of your opponents will never have read *any* books—and they won't play by them if they have. Some players have raising requirements that are far less stringent than others. Real maniacs often have no raising requirements at all; they're driven by nothing more substantial than ego and a whim.

Some players will raise with any suited ace in any position, as well as raise with hands like K-J, K-10, Q-J, J-10, and any pair of sixes or higher. Others—there aren't too many players like this, but there are a few—will raise with 10-7 offsuit just because they *have a hunch*. When you are playing against an opponent who raises with a very broad spectrum of hands, you won't necessarily be dominated if you hold an otherwise troublesome hand like A-J. In fact, the raiser might be the one who is dominated. While he may think otherwise, it just might be your foot that's firmly planted on his throat. There's no tactical edge more important than knowing your opponents. A hand like A-J, which should be released in the face of a raise from a sound player, might be a hand to reraise with against others.

You'll Win the Minimum but Lose the Maximum with Trouble Hands

Nevertheless, when you're holding a trouble hand, you'll seldom be sure whether you're in the lead or not. Because you have to consider that your hand might be dominated, you're apt to play passively by checking and calling rather than betting and raising. Even when you win these confrontations, caution minimizes the amount of your win. Your opponent—who seized the initiative with aggressive play—will maximize his or her wins.

File that thought away and don't lose touch with it. It's another example of why selective and aggressive play is a major factor underlying winning poker. It's also an example of the "know your opponents," line of reasoning. You know the mantra: Strategy often depends on the situation—and a hand that's playable against John might not be playable against Mary. When you're in early position, you won't know which of your opponents might come out firing. It could be Mary, the gal who never raises unless she holds a premium hand. But it might also be John, the maniac always on tilt who is just as likely to come after you with 7-6 or K-2 as he is with any other, more legitimate holding.

Ducking Trouble Hands

Here's how to deal with the unenviable consequences of finding your hand dominated by an opponent who also has the advantage of acting last, severely restricting the hands you play from early position. While face cards are pretty, they're not equally desirable. A hand like Q-J in early position—or even in middle position in an aggressive game—flings the door to domination wide open.

If you don't play hands that can get you in trouble, you won't find yourself staring up at *three-outers* and the improbable odds you'll have to overcome to win the pot. Although you cannot avoid dominated hands with 100 percent certainty—unless you refrain from playing all hands save a pair of aces—it's your first decision that matters most. If you are nimble enough to avoid getting yourself into this kind of trap in the first place, and both deft and sufficiently disciplined to extricate yourself from its clutches at the earliest hint of trouble, you'll find yourself doing just about anything to minimize the adverse impact of being dominated whenever you hold a troublesome hand.

This means that much of poker is about developing your senses to the point where you're able to realize when you've had the best of it. Exercise the sorely needed self-discipline required to release hands when you're staring up a long and lonely hill. If you can master this—and the skill required to execute this strategy is a lot tougher than any words we've used to describe it—the tactical aspects become pretty simple. This is particularly true when you're playing limit poker: Get your money into action when you have the best of it, and use your discipline to fold those dominated three-outers when you don't.

Putting Players on Hands

In tournaments and in cash games, from the moment the cards are in the air, start putting people on hands. Whether you personally decide to call or fold, keep a mental note on each player from the deal through the river. If players have to show their hands on the river, be sure to note whether or not you had originally made a correct assessment. Don't be afraid to change your opinion as the hand develops and you get more information. As soon as someone raises and the next person calls, you need to decide if the raiser is tight or loose and whether the caller has a big hand or is making a bad call. At that moment alone, who is winning? Do you think the caller knows the gap concept? Keep your initial assessments in mind when the flop comes and you are deciding whether each player is strong, weak, or bluffable. Will they beat the aggressor if they call? Make a bet with yourself. When you're out of the pot, who is going to win? If you're in the pot, you better be betting that you'll be the winner!

Even if future actions provide strong evidence to the contrary, many beginning players judge an opponent on a hand without ever revising the initial assessment. "You had K-Q of spades," a showoff, wannabe pro, tells his opponent. Usually it's tough or impossible to be that specific. Putting a player on a *range of hands* usually makes more sense, and, in fact, that's usually what's best to do.

In the instance cited above, a better assessment might be: "I put him on A-K, A-Q, K-Q, A-J, or a big pocket pair. But as he checked on the flop, when an ace fell, I knew he either had a pair smaller than aces or two high cards that did not contain an ace. He also might have flopped a set of aces and was *slow-playing* to set up a check-raise on a subsequent betting round. Since the odds made it far more likely that he had something other than a set of aces, I discounted that hand and acted accordingly."

Smooth Runs the Water Where the River Is Deep

Worry more about the player who calls than the player who bets—especially if the caller is tight or capable of trapping. This is even truer in a pot- or no-limit game. In either, there's no need to put the hammer down right away; you can always make a big bet on a later round. But if you have a very good hand, it generally pays to get some money in the pot, either by calling or betting a reasonable sum. This way opponents are lured into playing a pot on the cheap— or so they think—while you're slyly marrying them to their hand by having them invest so much in the pot. This leaves you in a wonderful position to take all their money with a bigger bet on the turn or the river.

Limpers

If a good player limps under the gun, watch out for pocket aces or other big pocket pairs. Note that most good players won't limp under the gun, especially in tournaments. If they do, they probably have a low pocket pair and are hoping to hit a set inexpensively, or a high pocket pair that they intend to trap you with, or maybe something like king/jack suited. If they have any of the weaker hands, they will fold in a tight game, if they're raised.

Learn to think like the other players. Why are they raising? Are they desperate? Do they trap? Are they straightforward?

A Call Can Be Scarier Than a Bet

Sometimes a call by a good player can be scarier than a raise. This is particularly true in a pot-limit or no-limit game when the board looks to be one that makes someone with a big hand.

If you bet in a pot- or no-limit game into a board of 7♦-

7♥5♥, or three suited cards, and your opponent just calls, be careful. He may have you lined up in his sights and he's getting ready to pull the trigger. If he wanted to drive you off the pot, he might make a large raise in an attempt to dissuade you from calling his bet. But by calling with a very big hand, he's accomplished a number of objectives.

First, he's gotten you to think he has a weak hand. If you believe that, you'll probably bet again on the next round. If you do come out betting, your opponent has you tied to the pot, which is now much larger—and a significant portion has come courtesy of your wagers.

If you're playing pot-limit, your opponent has now manipulated the size of the pot, albeit indirectly. That provides him with an opportunity to make a really big bet—one that puts your entire stack at risk.

Had he raised on your first bet, you might have read him for having a stronger hand and simply folded. However, this would have deprived him of a chance to win a large pot. By quietly calling with a powerhouse hand, he's giving you an opportunity to improve your own hand to one that's second best, tempting you to commit more chips to the pot.

Reading Minds

It helps to know some typical thoughts that run through the other players' heads at a table:

> "Hmm, someone just posted the blinds in addition to the usual blinds. That's lots of dead money in the pot. I think I'll go ahead and just raise with nothing to steal all that."

> "I have to make this bet on the river even though I missed my flush. It's the only way I can win this pot. If they reraise, I'll fold; otherwise, I just might win this pot."

Notice People's Betting Patterns

Who is cautious? Who is aggressive? Always review a player's hole cards against the cards on the board and his betting pattern. Is he careful? Does he bluff when he should or when he shouldn't? Does he call to keep his opponents honest, even though his hand is weak and has little chance of winning?

Notice All Hands Shown on the River

When you see players' hands on the river, rewind the tape in your head. What position did they play that in? How much did it cost them to call? Did they bet, raise, or simply call with that hand?

Watch Your Opponents

Are they getting ready to call or fold? Are the tells reliable or are they pretending they're going to call? Many players will hold their cards with their wrist cocked when preparing to fold—this is a very reliable tell. If you look to the left before it's your turn to act and see that your opponents look as though they're going to release their hands, you might wind up with the distinct advantage of being last to act. You'll then be able to raise into a group of players you knew were going to fold anyway. This will represent a very strong hand to your less observant adversaries.

Making Proper Assessments of Ability

You'll benefit the most from properly assessing your own level and abilities. If you were to take a poll of poker players and ask them whether they rated themselves below average, average, or above average, you'd find that the vast majority of players consider themselves better than average. But that can't be the case. Average, by definition, belongs square in the middle. Most players are average, or close to it. But the vast majority of them don't think so. Good players know how to take advantage of that.

The ability to make a personal assessment presupposes the skill and willingness to see oneself as others do. There's an old poker adage that says, "If you can't find the fish in the first fifteen minutes of sitting down at the table, you're it." And since being a *good* player is relative to the competition, if you are willing and able to assess your own skills in relation to those of your opponents, you can be selective. Pick games you're a favorite to beat; stay away from games in which you'd be a decided underdog. British author Anthony Holden, who took a year off to play the tournament circuit a few years ago, wrote a book called *Big Deal* about his experiences. He had this to say about self-awareness at the poker table: "Whether he likes it or not, a man's character is stripped bare at the poker table; if the other players read him better than he does, he has only himself to blame. Unless he is both able and prepared to see himself as other do, flaws and all, he will be a loser in cards, as in life."

Holden's observation is as clear as it is succinct. To determine your chances in any game, you need to be realistic in rating your own skill. You also should be able and willing to assess your abilities against those of your opponents. Within the massive self-delusion whereby most believe they are above average at poker resides a terrific opportunity for any player willing to bare his or her soul—but only to oneself. That is to make decisions based on the relative, realistic difference between oneself and the opposition.

Even Good Players Go on Tilt or Let Down Their Guard

No one is perfect—no one we know, anyway. Poker is a game that can grab you by the gut and slam you back into your chair with a near-physical force. Although you might make the right play while your opponent plays like a donkey, you can still lose the hand because of the fickle turn of a random card. Nothing can be done about it either, except to take it in stride and go on to the next hand. Nevertheless, it's easier said than done. When we get upset, we make bad decisions. Our guard is down and our opponents can read us with ease. Our advice here is that good players can control their emotions while weaker players frequently can't. Anyone aspiring to expert play can't allow himself to look disappointed or elated—unless he's setting up players to take notice of such things for a later sting operation. The key here is emotional control and control of how you present yourself at the poker table. Good acting skills are helpful, but you don't need to be Brando or Streep to pull off the job. All you have to be able to do is give your opponents reason to think you're going to zig, when you intend to zag.

Even Good Players Are Bad When They're Too Consistent

One player once said this about Sheree Bykofsky's play: "You can't put her on a hand because she mixes it up." That's a great compliment. Another poker compliment is when you are unwelcome at a poker table—even though you just bathed. When opponents fear you, when they can't read you or deduce your hand in any way, and they'd rather have another opponent that's a big advantage. When players are apprehensive about your skills, they're going to play differently against you, and usually they'll make some errors in judgment when they do. This amounts to a sizeable edge. And how do you achieve this level of skill? The secret is to play by the book most of the time, *but not always.*

Some players never play by the book because they've never read one. As a consequence they really have little idea of how to play in various common situations. Others play by the book so exclusively that reading their play is like following a recipe. You can almost see their hand by virtue of the fact that their play doesn't vary, and what they do in one situation today, they'll repeat every time that situation arises.

You don't have to vary by-the-book play all that often to plant the seeds of doubt in the minds of your opponents. Just make sure that they are observant enough to recall what you do. Then, once a session or so, provide variability in your game to create confusion on their part.

Go ahead and raise with your flush draw every now and then. If you make your hand and show it down, your opponents will think you're much more aggressive than you are. If you convey the impression of very tight play, don't do anything to disturb it. It's a license to bluff.

Dan Harrington, who won the World Series of Poker in 1995 and made the final table in 2003 and 2004, is known as "Action Dan." This is a tongue-in-cheek nickname that's been given to him because his image is that of a very tight player. But in the 2004 WSOP, a hand came up where Josh Arieh bet, eventual winner Greg Raymer raised, and Harrington reraised. Both Raymer and Arieh had shown a willingness to gamble a bit at the final table and call bets and raises from other players. But when Action Dan raised, both threw their hands away without much hesitation—testimony to Harrington's reputation for only betting when he has the goods. Imagine their surprise when they viewed the event on television and learned that Harrington stole a big pot right out from under their noses.

Only Harrington could have pulled this off. The same raise from another player would have engendered at least one call, and possibly two. But Action Dan had long established his reputation as a tight player and made his opponents pay because of it.

You Should Have Several Good Reasons for Every Decision

Have as many reasons as possible. And they need to be rational. Having a hunch doesn't count. Neither does some vague feeling that the cards were *due*. Cards are never due. They don't respond to hunches. They are inanimate objects made of plastic or cardboard with no intelligence or magical powers built into them. Cards are as dumb as dumb can be. Even a truckload of turnips looks like a Mensa convention compared to the cards at the poker table. Every pro knows this, so don't you forget it.

Learn Which Voice in Your Head Is the Most Reliable and Listen to It

Don't be afraid to tune out the mental noise that you know in your heart of hearts gives you bad information. Ignore all those false prophets rattling around inside your head. When you do this, you are almost guaranteed to be playing winning poker.

Position, Position, Position

Poker can be likened to that old real estate saw: The three most important concerns about buying a house are location,

location, and location. Well poker's no different. Location is important there, too. Only instead of calling it *location*, poker players refer to it as *position*.

As they say about hold'em on television's popular *World Poker Tour*, "It takes a minute to learn and a lifetime to master." A button goes around the felt in clockwise rotation, moving with each new deal. This gives each player in turn a chance to act last, thereby playing the best position. It also gives him a chance to play the worst position by acting first. Because poker is very much a game of position, rotating is very important. It keeps the game fair. And, although it's given lip service, that's the first tenet that most poker teachers understate when teaching the game.

Position in the betting order is so important that some hands worth a raise in late position should be folded quickly early in the betting order. After all, when you are forced to act early, you have no indication how many opponents plan to enter the pot with you. And no inclination whether any of them will represent a big hand by raising when it's their turn to act.

Good Position

When players talk about *good position*, they are usually referring to the advantages that accrue from acting last. Acting last gives you an opportunity to see what your opponents do before you have to decide whether you're willing to commit any money to the pot. You have some idea about the real or purported strength of their hand. When you act first, you are shooting in the dark. You don't know if your bet will cause all your opponents to fold, in which case you win the pot. It also will trigger a raise from someone who acts after you do and who has a big hand. You might even be raised by someone who figures you don't have a hand at all. Will his raise cause you to fold so he can win the pot?

There are two times when it's beneficial to act first. One is when you plan to bluff. Poker players are a skeptical bunch. When you bet from late or last position, after everyone else has checked, there's a natural tendency for your opponents to think you're trying to steal the pot. So, one or more of them might call to keep you honest.

Another time acting first is beneficial is when you have a powerful hand and are planning to check-raise. Of course, you should be certain that one of your opponents—preferably, the player to your immediate left—will bet if you check. If you check, and his bet attracts one or more callers, you can now check-raise and trap all of those callers for an additional bet.

But before you check-raise, two conditions have to be present. You have to have a very strong hand, and you have to believe that someone will bet. After all, it does you no good if you check and your opponents all check behind you. When that happens, rather than gaining an additional bet by check-raising, you'll lose a bet and give all of your opponents a free card in the process. Another time it does you no good is when you check-raise to a stronger hand than yours!

Position Is Critical to Winning Poker

Position is critical in poker, particularly in games like Texas hold'em and Omaha, where it's fixed for all four betting rounds. Position is so important that there are starting hands you can raise with when you're last to act that should be thrown away if you're in early position.

Suppose you're dealt a pocket pair of fives or a hand like A–9 or A–T. They're better than average hands, though not nearly in the same league as a pair of kings or aces. If you're last to act, or next to last—players refer to this as being in the cut-off seat—the action you take with hands like these will be based on how your opponents have played. If everyone has folded and the blinds are your only potential opponents, you probably have a better hand than either of them. After all, they each have *random* hands, and a pair of fives or a hand like A-9 or A-T figures to be better than average.

If you're following a prescription for winning poker by playing selectively and aggressively, this is the time to raise. Your opponents might fold, but even if they don't, you figure to have the best of it right now. It's always a good thing when your opponents call with lesser hands.

But what do you do if the pot is raised before it's your turn to act? If you examine your opponent's raising standards, chances are he will look for a hand that's bigger than a pair of fives or A-T before raising. A typical player probably has at least a pair of nines or A-J. If you decide to call, you're doing so with a lesser hand. That's not a good position to put yourself in.

Not only are you the underdog right now, but the cost to enter the pot is double what it was before your opponent's raise. And if you're playing no-limit, the cost might be a lot more than double the opening bet. Most no-limit players will make a "standard" raise of three to four times the blind. In a no-limit game, your standards for calling a raise—or reraising once someone else has raised before it's your turn to act—need to be elevated to overcome the high cost of competing. If you are going to call a raise, or make it three bets to go in a no-limit game, you ought to be darn sure you are the favorite in this hand.

Many players seem dismayed when they have to release a hand such as 5-5 or A-T in the face of a raise. After all, they were looking forward to playing it. But when you play poker, money saved is just as valuable as money won. Throwing away a vulnerable hand saves money you figured to lose. This is because you are confronting an opponent whose hand figures to be stronger than yours.

Acting last, or in late position, has saved you money by providing you with information. You used it to make a more informed decision. If you played your pocket pair of fives in early position, where you had little or no information about the real or purported strength of your opponent's hand and then had to deal with a raise behind you, chances are you would be swimming upstream. Poker is a game of incomplete information to be sure, and the information you receive when you act last, or in late position, is usually a lot better than what's at your disposal when you're flying blind. This is because you don't have the benefit of knowing what course of action any of your opponents have chosen.

When you have to act early in the betting order, you're forced to consider the strength of your own hand in a vacuum. But poker is not a game of absolute values; it's a game of relative values. You can win some hands with ace-high, while others will take a full house or better to capture the pot. And when you have no idea about your opponent's holdings, you cannot possibly relate the quality of your hand to the purported strength of his, and that's a major disadvantage.

Position Betting

The feel of the flop induces or inhibits betting. Professional poker players always realize that the flop's texture can induce or inhibit betting. Some flops just look like they help people, while others never seem to help anyone. Some flops,

however, are so portentous, that they appear to have pro-
duced a hand so big for the first person who bets into it,
that almost no one will call. Here are some examples:

A really ragged flop such as 7-3-2 figures to help no one
except the blinds, and that's only if they're in a pot that
wasn't raised. No one in his right mind will voluntarily see
the flop with cards connecting with these dogs. The exception would be on those rare occasions when someone plays
a hand such as A-7 suited, or a pair of sevens, for one bet.

A flop with two or three face cards figures to help a lot
of players. After all, hold'em is a big-card game, and most
players who voluntarily enter pots do so with hands containing pairs or big cards. A flop such as A-Q-J can provide
something for everyone, or almost everyone who has seen
the flop. When that happens, the question isn't how much
the flop helped you, but how well it helped your opponent.

Sometimes you'll see a flop such as J-T-9 suited. In this
case, someone might have made a flush, another player
might have a straight, or someone else might have two pair
or a pair with a straight or a flush draw. Even a straight
flush is possible. When that happens, most players who
haven't been helped in a big way by the flop are likely to
fold at the first sign of a bet. The same goes for when the
flop is 8-8-8. Only someone with an eight, or another pair,
or an ace in his hand, is likely to continue playing. After
all, even a full house is dead in the water if an opponent
happens to have the fourth eight in his hand.

Texture is critical in determining how your hand stacks
up vis-à-vis your opponents' hands. But when you examine
a flop's texture, do what the pros all do: Examine it in light
of your opponents' playing styles and a firm knowledge of
the kinds of cards they are likely to hold in their hands. If a
tight player is not in the blind, you can be certain that a
ragged flop did not help him. Other players, those who call

with almost anything, can be helped by almost any flop. Nevertheless, the texture of a flop can go a long way to helping you assess whether your opponent really has a hand or not.

The Rules Are the Same, but the Game Is Dramatically Different at Different Betting Limits

This is similar to the analogy between tournament and cash game poker, which are like two different games. The higher up you go in betting limits, the better your opponents figure to be. While you'll occasionally run into some appallingly bad players who can afford to play high-stakes poker and enjoy it whether they win or lose, most of the time bigger games are tougher games. You'll find fewer players in each pot because players at this level have learned to be selective. You'll also find more raises because they've learned to be aggressive, too.

In a passive, low-limit game, where most of the players who enter a pot come in calling, position is not as important as it is in a game where raising is the order of the day. After all, if you can see the flop for one bet, you're in almost as good a shape from early position as you are if you're the last to act. But not in an aggressive, higher-limit game. Many players have difficulty making the transition from lower betting limits to higher-limit games.

Why Adjustments Are Necessary When You Move Up in Limits

In order to make an adjustment to bigger games, you'll need to be sensitive to the relationship between pot odds and the odds against hitting your hand. You'll also need to learn how to deduce what hands your opponents might have by correlating their betting patterns against the hands they show down. And while you're scrutinizing your opponents, be on the lookout for their bluffing frequencies. Do they bluff often, or seldom? When they do bluff, is it predicated on scare cards, such as three-suited cards coming on the board? Do they also seem to bluff by representing very unlikely hands? Be observant. The best time to do this is when you're not involved in a hand.

Studying Your Opponents

Wise players make use of the time they're not actively involved in hands to study opponents. This is the best and most profitable method of raising your game to the next level. While the rules of poker are the same regardless of the betting limits, the game seems different and, in fact, is different at higher limits in terms of game texture, the degree of aggression by most of your opponents, and the selectivity and craftiness of the players.

The More Betting Patterns You Know, the More You'll Win

A thorough knowledge of betting patterns is just one element in a poker player's toolbox, but it may be the most important. Betting patterns can help you track the playing styles of your adversaries. They can also help you analyze some parts of your own game that may need improvement. What's the most common pattern you'll find in a hold'em game? It goes like this: call, bet, bet, check. You've seen your opponents do this all the time and probably do it yourself. You call the blinds before the flop, catch a good hand—something like top pair with a good kicker—so you bet the flop and bet the turn, too. But when you fail to improve to three-of-a-kind or two pair, you decide to check the river to save a bet just on the odd chance that you're beaten.

Players Leave Money on the Table by Failing to Bet the River

If this describes your play, you're leaving money on the table. Most of the time the river card is not going to promote your opponent's hand to one that's better than yours, as long as you've had the best hand going into the river. If you have the luxury of acting last, and the river card doesn't spell "flush" or "straight" for one of your opponents, go ahead and bet. You're likely to be safe, not sorry, if you do. Even if the last card puts three cards of the same suit on the board, any player fortunate enough to catch his flush card on the river usually comes out betting when it's his turn to act. And if he had a bigger hand than yours before the river—suppose he flopped a set, or the top two pair—well, sure as we're sitting here, he'll do his check-raising on the turn, not the river.

Best Hands Tend to Hold Up from the Turn to the River

What's the message in this bottle? Every pro knows this, but surprisingly, not too many amateurs are aware of it. Most of the times you have the best hand on the turn, you stand a very good chance of having the best hand on the river, and you ought to bet. If you habitually check the river with a hand like top pair, good kicker, you are leaving money on the table. You're also not doing much for your image, either. But this is about as easy a fix as there is in anyone's poker game. Just bet the river. That's all there is to it. Change your betting pattern from call, bet, bet, check, to this pattern: call, bet, bet, bet, and see for yourself.

Big-Hand Betting Patterns

Here's another common betting pattern: Call, check/call, check-raise, bet. This is the hallmark of a player with a good hand. Perhaps he's flopped a set, or two pair, or even an ace to his A-K. So he checks and calls when someone else bets the flop, and then check-raises the turn in hopes of trapping an opponent or two for a few bets. Then he continues to drive the hand by betting the river. There's nothing unusual here. You've done it yourself, and this is probably the most common betting pattern employed by players holding big hands. They quietly call the flop in hopes of getting in a check-raise on the turn; then they bet out on the river.

So when you see the pattern of check/call followed by a check-raise on the turn, credit your opponent with a big hand that's probably better than yours. While you might find some extraordinarily creative players who will check-raise-bluff every now and then, it doesn't happen all that often in most games, and almost never at lower limits. When you're the victim of a check/call, check-raise betting pattern, go ahead and throw your hand away unless you've got an extraordinarily strong hand or a draw at the right price to a better hand than your opponent is likely to be holding.

The Cost of Stubborn Play Is Usually Two Bets

Many players are reluctant to throw away a hand to a check-raise. As a result of their stubborn nature, they lose a big bet on the turn and another on the river. And they needn't do this. After all, most of the time that you're check-raised, your opponent has the better hand. And most of the time, if he exhibits this betting pattern, you should do the smart thing. Throw your hand away. If you do, you will have saved two bets. And money saved is equal to money won. Even if you are a consistently winning player who averages one big bet in the plus column per hour, calling a check-raise when you strongly suspect you are beaten will take two hours of play to recoup. When Kenny Rogers was singing, "You gotta know when to fold'em," that was his message.

What Other Common Betting Patterns Can Reveal About Your Opponents

These aren't the only betting patterns to be aware of. If you see someone play the pattern characterized by betting or raising and then folding, you've got an opponent who is sufficiently disciplined to throw away hands like a pair of jacks to an overcard. He might also get rid of Big Slick when the flop is small, and there's some action by other players, before it's his turn to act.

Another pattern to be aware of is this one: bet, bet, check, and either check, bet, call, or raise on the river. This pattern marks a player who takes a free card when the circumstances suit him, and you can mark him as a tough, disciplined foe.

Check, call, bet is a pattern you don't see all that often. This usually happens when you check a flop that looks very ragged and doesn't figure to have helped either your opponent or you. When your opponent bets, you call behind him. This creates the illusion that you either are a compulsive caller with no hope of winning the pot, or you did get some part of the flop, or you picked up a draw and are justified in continuing on in the hand.

If your opponent sees you as a solid player and not a calling station, he'll probably go with the latter of the two possibilities. Now, regardless of whether the turn card helps you or not, you can come out betting. If a smallish card falls, your opponent may think you've made a straight or that you have two pair. If all he has is two overcards, he's likely to throw them away. On the other hand, if a big card falls that does not help your opponent, he's likely to give you credit for calling on the flop with two overcards, hitting one of them on the turn. Now you have a top pair with a big kicker. If he cannot beat that, he's likely to fold. Although this is a strong play, it will only work against opponents good enough and disciplined enough to throw away a hand they were betting, or even raising, because your betting pattern convinced them that you have a superior hand. On the other hand, if you try this ploy against a perpetual caller, you will only win when you get lucky and catch your card; you will never be able to drive him off whatever hand he has. In fact, he may be blissfully ignorant of your betting pattern. He may not even realize that you were sending him a message.

Drawing Hands

If you're drawing, draw only to the nuts. The worst feeling is to hit your flush and to lose to a higher flush. And be especially careful when drawing to straights. It is no secret why they call the bottom end of a straight the idiot end. You will feel like an idiot if the ten gives you a straight to the King while giving your opponent a straight to the ace.

Redraws

It's always helpful to have more than one way to win, and redraws provide that opportunity. A redraw occurs when you've made one hand with a draw for a better one. The example provided by Michael Wiesenberg in *The Official Dictionary of Poker* shows a player starting with 8♥ 9♥, and flopping a flush when the board is 2♥ T♥ J♥. Not only does our hero have a flush, he also has a redraw for a straight flush.

There's no mystery here. Flopping a hand like a flush is nice, but you'd ideally like to have the cards that give you a draw to a straight flush, too. While your flush may hold up, the presence of three suited cards will also keep any opponent who has one big card of that suit in the pot and drawing to a flush. Imagine his surprise if he makes his hand only to find out that you not only flopped a flush, but you also redrew to a bigger hand and beat him.

Sometimes, you'll flop a set only to have your opponent make a straight or flush on the turn. But if the board pairs, your set now becomes a full house or quads, and you will have redrawn on him. This does not happen too often in hold'em, but redraws are a common occurrence in Omaha and Omaha/8.

Playing the River

Sometimes big revelations come from small insights and occur so quickly that you don't even notice them. "I'm losing on the river most of the time I call," Lou was told by someone who decided to chat him up at a local casino.

"Most of the time I call a bet on the river, I lose," he said, adding, "I know I'm stubborn, but I just don't like to let go of a hand when I go that far with it. Besides, if my opponent bets and he's bluffing, I'll lose the entire pot when I fold, but it only costs me one additional bet to call that last bet."

Why Calling a Bet on the River
Is the Error of Choice

It's true that if you *must* make an error on the river, calling should be the error of choice. The price of a call is only one additional bet; the cost of releasing the winning hand in the face of an opponent's wager can be ten bets or more, depending on the size of the pot. Because of the potential cost associated with folding what would have been the winning hand, it's a huge error instead of a small, incremental one. Nevertheless, that doesn't mean that a bet on the river should always be called. There are some occasions when it pays to toss your hand away when confronted with one last bet.

But that's not what this discussion was all about. To Lou, it seemed like there was a lot more beneath the surface than deciding to call or fold when confronted with a bet on the river. Something else was at play here, and that's when he had an epiphany of sorts.

All of us aren't going to the river with equal hands, and the circumstances where we find ourselves confronting a bet on the river are very different. Our hero—who seemed to be the caller more often than not while losing much of the time—isn't just making a mistake on the river, he's probably making a mistake on the turn, too.

Potential Versus Realized Value

Lou's mind flashed back to his last session. In six-plus hours of playing, he called twice on the river with hands that lost. The rest of the time, he was the bettor on the river and won without a call, or won when called by an opponent, or the hands were checked down at the end and a winner was determined. Lou also threw his hand away on a draw that never materialized, and he couldn't even beat a decent bluff, or he wasn't contesting the river at all.

The river plays itself much of the time. You've either made two pair, a set, or better, or completed a flush or straight draw. You think that that top pair with a big kicker is good enough to win if you bet and are called. You could also have a hand that's a candidate for checking down at the end. While there are some occasions when you'll want to bluff an opponent who is prone to releasing marginal holdings, when faced with a bet on the river, those are the only exceptions.

Much of the time decisions on the river are not all that tough. Your hand has either realized its potential or it's failed to do so. In any event, it no longer has any potential and you can neither bet nor call because you *hope* your hand will improve on some future betting round. At this point you've either made the hand you were hoping to make or you didn't—and if you made it, you should bet. After all, if you're building a hand but are unwilling to bet if you complete it, why are you attempting to make that hand in the first place? There's no payoff for sticking around in hopes of building the second or third best hands. You want to draw to hands that will win the pot, not lose it.

An Error on the River Is Often an Indication of Blundering on the Turn and the Flop, Too

The river isn't the key to any of this. Whenever a mistake is made on the river, there's a good chance that it's merely compounding a mistake made on an earlier betting round. Remember our hero, the guy who was calling and losing with regularity on the river? The river's probably not his undoing at all. Maybe it's the turn. If he looks back at the hands he's played, he'll probably see that he shouldn't have played them on the turn either.

And if he made an error on the turn, perhaps he shouldn't have called a bet on the flop. And, yes, he probably had a hand that didn't warrant a play before the flop either. The answers can be as varied as the player and his cards, but if you're finding yourself calling and losing too often on the river, you need to examine the way your hand played out and decide if you should have been involved with it on the turn. But don't stop there. Go back to the flop and even the start of the hand.

You might be making mistakes on one or more of these betting rounds, and these errors are leading you down the wrong road. Then you find yourself at the river, confronted by an opponent's wager. You decide to call in order to avoid the catastrophic dilemma of folding a winning hand. But the river is not your problem. It only seems like the problem because the river is where the results are revealed—and there's nowhere to go from there but onto the next hand. But the truth of the matter is that the river is only the last visible symptom of an issue that developed far earlier.

Look at the hands you're losing with and look backwards with an eye toward deciding where you should have gotten off the train. You might have been better off exiting at the turn, or quite possibly, a whole lot earlier than that.

The Best Hold'em Hands Usually Hold Up

In poker in general, and especially in Texas hold'em, the best starting hand becomes the winning hand more often than not. Calling with hands that build second or third pair or long-shot holdings like small-gapped connectors are hands that frequently put you on the road to ruin. When you do win with them, no one will suspect that you have such beauties in your hand. But in limit hold'em, they don't win enough money to provide a long-term positive expected value. Save those hands for no-limit games, where you can see the flop for one bet with lots of opponents in the pot and you're getting nearly infinite implied odds. If you can manage your impulses, so that you can release these hands whenever they don't flop an absolutely miraculous hand for you—which will be the vast majority of the time—then you can play them.

But if you're losing too frequently at the river, just try backing up. You'll probably find that your real error occurred a lot earlier in the game.

The Big Picture

Don't forget that to win at poker requires a confluence of many factors. If you have the best hand you have to play it right. You have to hit the board and you have to have the best hand after the river. And you have to get the players with better hands to fold. Therefore, you *must* be able to release excellent hands—even aces. Some of the best players measure their success not by the hands they've played but by the hands they've folded.

Unreality TV

The majority of new players who have become hooked on poker by watching it on TV are seeing something that's not really there. Anyone who tries to learn the game in this way is in for a rude awakening in the real world. TV truncates the game. The viewer gets to watch only the exciting hands, the big bluffs, the tough lay-downs, and they get to see every hand face up. Plus, the commentary is often misleading. The commentators sometimes say, "I wonder why he thought so long, Mike," without ever referencing pot odds or the size of the blinds. But most of poker is not made up of this at all. Most of poker is routine to mundane, and straightforward play generally carries the day.

The current fascination with poker is guaranteed to accomplish two things: First, it will send droves of new players into casinos and card rooms everywhere, just aching to be dealt in. Second, if they learned their poker from watching TV, they learned wrong!

How can that be? If they watch how top pros like Phil Ivey, Howard Lederer, and the legendary Doyle Brunson play, why will the TV audience be learning incorrectly? Won't those bold calls and larcenous bluffs, the kind that seemingly work so well on TV, work in your neighborhood card room, too?

"The Medium Is the Message," but a Plasma TV Is Not a Poker Table

The answer, in a word, is "No!" The reason it won't work can be found in the observations of Marshall McLuhan, the University of Toronto professor who first told the world, "The medium is the message." In so doing he revolutionized the way we view and understand communications. Well, McLuhan may never have played a hand of poker in his life—we don't know for sure—but his observation was spot-on. According to McLuhan, the nature of the medium through which a message is conveyed—whether it be through newspaper, television, or radio—was as significant as the context of the message itself. He saw media as an extension of mankind, much the same as our voices and our ability to put pen to paper are extensions of ourselves. A Marine drill instructor moves his troops with a booming, commanding voice, while Marilyn Monroe got a very different message across in little-girl, sexy, come-hither tones.

To put McLuhan's theory in poker terms: What TV-watching poker newbies haven't grasped is the enormous difference between tournament poker—particularly no-limit, short-handed games of five players or fewer—and full ten-player limit hold'em cash games. After all, when the blinds represent a fairly significant part of each player's equity in a tournament, you just can't sit around and wait for a big-pocket pair or Big Slick before firing some chips at the pot. If you wait, you'll bleed to death.

Poker newbies usually don't realize that limit poker, played as a cash game with tiny blinds at a full table requires a store of patience to wait for good hands. Short-handed tournament poker—where the blinds become astronomical and too much patience is a terminal disease—requires a lot more risk-taking. This is the end of the spectrum where the selection-aggression quotient leans heavily toward aggressive play. On TV, any hand, with an ace in it, or any pair in hand, is raised most of the time. In a full table, low-limit cash game at your neighborhood card room, it takes a lot more than that. But those seduced by poker on the telly haven't grasped that point—and won't if watching television is their only means of learning the game.

In Long Tournaments, It's Survival Early, Aggression Later

In tournaments, aggression very gradually increases over the course of the event. It's sort of like revving up an automobile engine, except it's done over a much longer period of time. In really long events, such as the $10,000 no-limit hold'em tournament at the World Series of Poker—which takes nearly a week to complete—the experts have one goal only for the first few days: They want to survive. They aren't revving up their aggression engines early at all, and they're not out to take every risk possible in hopes of gathering all the chips that they might win. They merely want to survive the first few days and put themselves into position to compete for all the marbles later in the week. They've learned that you can't win a tournament in the early stages. You can lose it, but it can't be won until the end stages.

Another common mistake made by those who have learned poker only by watching short-handed, final table tournaments on TV is overvaluing small and medium pairs in cash games. When the blinds come 'round with regularity because there are only five players at the table—and they're so high that one just can't outwait them in the hopes of finding a big hand—small and medium pairs have to be played strongly.

If you wake up with a pair of eights, or even a pair of sixes in a short-handed tournament, it's a raising hand surely. But when you're at a full table in a cash game, particularly at lower limits, where almost everyone will call regardless of what you do, those small and medium pocket pairs will probably be looking at overcards on the flop. And at least one of your opponents figures to have a better hand than yours. In a full game, smaller pairs need to flop a set to retain their value. In a short-handed tournament, a big raise from a pocket pair stands a good chance of forcing your opponents to fold. If, perchance, you're called by someone with a hand like A-K or A-Q, what the heck—you're a small favorite anyway as long as you're up against a lone opponent.

When you're short-handed in a tournament, you can raise with a pretty dicey hand, as long as no one else has entered the pot. And once you raise, your opponents will need fairly strong hands to risk what amounts to a significant portion of their tournament equity to call. There's a big chasm between raising hands and calling hands in tournaments, particularly when those raises represent a major chunk of *your* change. In a nine-handed cash game, where you can buy more chips anytime you go broke on a hand, you'll find players who call with hands they wouldn't dream of playing if they were skilled tournament pros and were short-handed at the final table.

When you're watching poker on TV, the announcers only intermittently tell you how many chips each player has or what one person's chip stack is relative to another's at a particular moment. Moreover, they almost never inform you as to what the different color chips are worth. Most important, they don't even tell you what the blinds are during a given hand! These are essential facts for players to keep in mind during each and every moment of the game—particularly at the final table of a tournament.

These aren't the only errors made by newbies who have learned their poker simply by watching it on TV. But they are among the most egregious. You'll find others, too. Poker on TV, dealt up short-handed in a tournament format, is not a low-limit cash game in your neighboring casino. Differences between these two forms of poker are as different as Arena Football is to the NFL and miniature golf is to the PGA tour. And when one mimics the style of game that's tailored to one medium but not the other, the results can be catastrophic.

As long as new players keep walking into casinos, however, there's a winning opportunity for skilled players. And when those newbies are convinced that the kind of chops they've seen on TV will play just as well in an entirely different game environment, well, you really can't ask for more than that, can you?

It's Exhausting to Play Good Poker

The person reading *Card Player* at the table instead of studying the game is at a great disadvantage. Not only does it benefit you to be *working* at the table, you also can take an unobservant player's money, too. Poker is a game of incomplete information, and we're forced to make decisions with less than all the facts. But incomplete information doesn't mean there's no information. There's lots of information just waiting to be picked up at the card table. But we have to be observant to gather those pearls of wisdom and that means staying in the game all of the time—when we're not in a hand as well as when we're involved in a pot. In fact, you're much more likely to pick up tells and tidbits of usable information from other players when you're not involved in a hand. This is when you can afford to concentrate exclusively on the other players, rather than having to process information and make a decision about your own hand.

So if you're the one reading the sports pages at the poker table, you're eschewing the chance to gather lots of useful intelligence you can use to win an additional pot here and there. Moreover, your more astute opponents know that when you're reading, you're not playing your best poker either.

If You Don't Study Your Opponents Whenever You Can, You're at a Big Disadvantage Compared to the Players Who Do

All the pros know that an ability to read one's opponent is important. But you can't read a player as though you're turning pages in a book. Information you become aware of at the poker table needs to be interpreted in light of how well you know your opponent. One person's meat, as the proverb goes, is another one's poison. Scrutinize your opponents—either online, where you're taking notes, or in a brick-and-mortar casino—so you can correlate that knowledge with the hand he turns up at the showdown.

The information is there, free of charge, for the observant and dedicated player to glean and use. But knowledge is only relevant when it's particularized to your opponent. That's why the answer to so many poker questions is, "It depends."

If you want to give yourself the biggest edge you can, pay attention to the game. The best time to do this is when you're *not* involved in a hand. If you're playing online, be sure and keep good notes about your opponents. If you're in a traditional casino, you can get up from the table or even make notes there. When you're not involved in a hand, build a book on your adversaries. You'll be glad you did.

Eating and Sleeping Well Magically Makes Your Cards Better

Being in the zone. Zen playing. Increased patience. Broccoli makes the brain function better than donuts. Drinking water is better than drinking wine. Poker requires a heightened state of alertness. When involved in a hand, you have to be alert to your cards and your opponents' actions. You also need to develop an awareness of what others at the table think *you* might be holding. Occasionally, one of your opponents will take an action or make a gesture that just doesn't square with the sense you have of what's going on in the game. When that happens, when you know something's going on but just can't figure it out, don't make the mistake of ignoring it just because you can't pinpoint where it belongs in the puzzle. Keep on the lookout and try to determine what that message might mean in light of any further betting, calling, raising, or folding. What does it mean in the light of the hands that are shown down at hand's end?

You may not always be able to piece every part of the puzzle together. But the more you work at it, the more likely you are to expand your knowledge of an opponent. You will also improve your broader ability to synthesize information from seemingly unrelated pieces of data—and that's one of the marks of an expert poker player.

If awareness is the hallmark of a champion, sensitivities that are switched off will downgrade your game significantly. Anything that dulls the senses can and probably will hurt you at the poker table. That includes alcohol, too much food, the wrong food, as well as external factors like too little sleep, concerns about personal issues unrelated to poker, battling the flu, or fighting with your spouse. If you aren't prepared to play at your best level, it's a good time to go to the movies, do some chores, or anything else you can accomplish on autopilot. The game's not going anywhere. Regardless of whether you play in a casino or in cyberspace, the game will always be there when you're ready for it.

While there are lots of winning poker styles—one can be the aggressor, the trapper who allows aggressive opponents to do his betting for him, or the counterpuncher, the list goes on. But if you're not playing your best, and are not in touch with your normally fine-tuned senses, your chances of winning are greatly reduced.

How Life Is Both Like and Unlike a Poker Game

There's not a poker pundit anywhere who has not observed that the lessons of poker and the lessons of life are remarkably similar. Both the real world and poker require participants to make decisions on incomplete information, be observant about our clients and colleagues, take calculated risks, control our emotions, bluff on occasion, maintain an image and a game face, and take advantage of fortune whenever it favors us. But life and poker are not identical. It's hard to function effectively in society if you develop a reputation as a liar or an inveterate bluffer. And the idea of beneficent giving is unheard of in poker.

While the ability to deceive can be used to great advantage at the poker table, it's a mixed blessing in the real world. The con man that deceives people in order to get his hands on their money is reviled. But little white lies are necessary in order to smooth social interaction. After all, when someone says, "How are you?" they're not really interested in hearing a litany of all your woes. What do you tell a spouse who asks, "Do I look fat in this"? The only answer one can give is, "Absolutely not; you look spectacular!"

The real world is a bit more complicated than life at the poker table. Nevertheless, poker does serve as a good model for life. We'll explain where the metaphor fits and where some adjustments are needed to view life as a poker game.

As in life, sometimes you only get one chance to do the right thing. Sometimes you'll even get two chances, but you rarely get three. If you are lucky enough to get a second chance, don't blow it! That goes for life and poker.

Woo-woo. If you go to the gym in the morning, later that day someone will send you flowers out of the blue. The universe has a way of rewarding good choices—sometimes as a direct result of your actions and sometimes not. The same is true in poker. Make the right decisions and you'll experience a little more than your share of luck, which will help you along the rest of the way.

In life and in poker, if you're polite, professional, polished, patient, powerful, and in good position, plenty of success will follow.

In poker, as in life, when you see challenge as an opportunity, you'll improve every difficult experience and reap unimaginable rewards. After all, when you've accomplished something that at first seemed difficult or impossible, it is infinitely more satisfying than simply doing something that comes easy to you.

If You Want Something Done, Do It Yourself

When you're in late position and you've bet or raised pre-flop, many players will expect you to do their raising for them. Don't do other people's betting—unless you're trapping them. Bet and raise only when you think it's to your own advantage. If you think someone is limping with the intent to check-raise or bet into you later, as Mike Caro would say, "Disappoint them."

Keep Your Options Open

Poker is like riding in a cab. If you're a smart cab driver, you won't work a street without an exit. It's better to leave your options open, turning when the lights and traffic are favorable to you. Same with poker. Keep your options open. Be ready to get out of a bad situation. Step on the gas when the coast is clear.

Don't Educate

When an obvious newbie sits down at the table and asks, "How much can I bet?" or "What's a chop?" all of the good players at the table will keep the information to themselves and rush to exploit it. The second-best players will exchange knowledgeable winks at each other, silently communicating that the new person will surely walk away chipless. The least skillful players at the table will start complaining, "You played jack three in middle position; what are you, a moron?" Another slightly better player will invariably chastise, "Don't educate the players at the table." Everyone will pray the newbie doesn't take offense and run away. Anyone who does more than take in the information about everyone and act accordingly is playing less than great poker. Don't tap on the aquarium walls; if you do, those metaphorical fish at the table will likely take notice and dart off in some other direction.

Planning Ahead

Any time you're involved in a pot that is raised before the flop, remember, it's going to get expensive. Even if the pre-flop raiser flops nothing, he's going to posture raise, reraise and bet. You're going to have to flop the nuts or fold.

Protecting Your Hand

When you play seven-card stud a double-sized bet is permitted on fourth street if someone has a pair showing. This allows anyone holding a pair to protect his hand. Although far more people are playing Texas hold'em these days instead of stud, many poker players still think of protecting one's hand in these terms: Betting out the maximum allowable, so that anyone thinking of chasing your pair down has to think twice because the price just doubled. But there's much more to protection than that. After all, sometimes you want to knock out certain callers while encouraging others to pay the price in order to chase you.

Manipulating the Odds in No-Limit and Pot-Limit Games

This happens all the time in no-limit and pot-limit games where you have the latitude of manipulating the size of the pot by the size of your bet. When you do this correctly, you can control the pot odds offered to your opponent—the very odds he must consider in relation to the odds against making his hand before he decides to call. That's something you can't do in a limit game.

Let's say you flopped top set in a no-limit game, but the board contains two hearts. No one knows you've flopped a set. Only you do. You can bet whatever you have in front of you. Because this is a theoretical example, we'll assume that you have millions stacked up in front of you and that the pot is small by comparison. If the pot is a couple of hundred—or even a couple of thousand dollars—it doesn't make a difference when you have a million dollars or more at your disposal. If you push all your chips into the pot, you're probably not going to be called. If you are, your opponent is likely to have the nuts with a redraw to an even bigger hand. Nevertheless, if you bet some trifling, minis-cule amount, you can count on being called by anyone with a draw who is hoping that a bargain-basement miracle completes his hand. And while he's doing this, an imagi-nary cash register in his mind is tallying up all the money he's hoping to win when those implied odds are realized.

A Theoretical Optimal Bet

Both of these polar extremes can hurt you. But somewhere in the middle is a bet size that will accomplish its objective: Drive out all the draws that might beat you and encourage those holding lesser hands to call. While you're sitting there deciding what to do with your set, you should be trying to land squarely on that theoretical betting amount. It should not permit drawing hands to overcome the cost of the draw, while encouraging anyone else with top pair, or two pair, to call.

The size of that precise betting amount is subject to a number of contingencies, including how willing your opponents are to take the worst of it in trying to run you down. At a minimum, the size of your bet needs to be sufficiently sized to reduce the payoff odds to less than 1.86-to-1—the odds against making a flush draw. If you bet enough money so that your opponent is only getting a bit more than 1-to-1, you've manipulated the pot odds to a point where he can't logically call your bet.

Aggressive Play Can Protect Your Hand

Another form of protecting your hand comes into play whenever you flop a straight or flush draw and your hand contains overcards to the flop. If you have A♥T♥, the flop is 9♥6♦3♥, and since there's a bet and a couple of callers with players still to act after you do, you ought to think about raising if anyone bets into you. Many players will not consider this because they fear chasing away "customers" if they make a flush. That's okay if the pot is small, but if it's nicely sized, try to win it now. Anytime you are able to eliminate opponents, your chances of winning the pot will improve.

While eliminating opponents won't make your nut flush any more likely to come in, fewer opponents may allow you to win even if you miss your flush but pair your ace or ten. Raising also brings more money into the pot, albeit from fewer players, and that's to your advantage. By eliminating opponents, some of your outs—other than those to the flush—become more effective. A pair of aces with a ten kicker might hold up to win the pot against two or three opponents, but it stands a smaller chance against a larger field. The cost of all this strategically adroit aggressive play is just one bet, and it's a small price to pay for an increased likelihood of winning the pot.

While the idea of "protecting your hand" seems defensive—the word "protection" connotes defending something and sounds inherently passive—hand protection in poker is anything but. When you bet out or raise you are protecting your hand via a preemptive strike, and there's nothing passive about it. Our advice to you is simple: KO your opponents now, before they have a chance to slide into the fray on the cheap and draw out on you.

What Makes Poker a Game You Can Beat?

The fact that the odds are always shifting in poker, and that you don't have to play a hand to its conclusion just because you called a bet or two on earlier rounds, is what enables good players to win at poker. You don't have this option in casino table games, and that's the reason you can win at poker. Never figure to be able to beat craps, roulette, baccarat, and other such games, where the odds are fixed and set to favor the house.

When playing casino table games, you make a bet and for the most part that bet is still working until the particular confrontation you've wagered on has ended. And even if there is a surrender option, guess who figures to get the best of this deal, you or the house?

In poker you have the ability to opt in and opt out. It's often the ability and willingness to fold your tent and steal away into the night—saved money clutched tightly in your hot little hands—that provides the resources allowing you to play another hand when you have the best of it.

We know you came to play. And getting involved in a hand and slugging it out with the guys and gals at the table is a lot more fun than sitting on the sidelines. But that's what you have to do most of the time to be a winning player. Watch the good players. They'll play far fewer hands than you do. If you don't believe us, clock them and see for yourself. It only seems like they're always in there slugging because they play very aggressively whenever they do enter a pot, and that's what you remember. But the one play they make above all others is the simplest and most boring in poker. They fold.

The One Who Folds the Most Wins the Most

When you first sit down at a poker table, it is important to assess the players as soon as possible. Who is winning, who is losing, what are their unique playing styles? Who plays well, who plays straightforwardly or by the book, who traps, who is cautious, who plays too many hands, who is aggressive? Most importantly, who has the chips? Inevitably, you'll see a busy table with lots of banter, bluffing, raising, reraising, mulling over, and staring down. There's one player with no chips reading *Bluff* or *PokerPro*, another one wolfing down ravioli with smelly Parmesan cheese—and there'll be one player almost hidden behind Fort Chip. She has ten stacks of forty chips each neatly arranged side by side. She's peering out intensely but serenely above the stack, watching the goings on with much interest. You're scratching your head over her because you can sit there for quite a while and never see her play a hand. But when you blink, look away and turn back, she's raking in another gigantic pot and neatly arranging her eleventh stack. This is the player who folds the most. Provided she's not too tight a player, you want to be this player. Isn't that why you're playing? To win? The one who folds the most wins the most.

Winning Money Is Important; Winning Pots Isn't

Remember, the objective of poker is to win money, not to win pots. If you want to win the most pots, that's easy. Just play every hand until the bitter end or until you can see you're beaten on board and you'll win every pot it was possible for you to win. It's a guarantee that by evening's end you'll be the one who won the most pots. But unless you were having an incredible run of cards, you're also the one most likely to have gone broke.

The one doing the most folding plays a much different style of poker than the person trying to win the most pots. The former is selective and aggressive. The latter may be aggressive or passive, but he's anything but selective. Winning poker requires combining selectivity with aggression, all in the right proportion. The proper mix depends on the game, your opponents, how well they play, whether they are too passive or too aggressive, and how they view your playing style. A lot of what goes into establishing the right proportion is more an art than a recipe, but much of it can be learned.

Fold Most of the Time

When you're playing Texas hold'em, or any other form of poker for that matter, you'll be folding most of the hands dealt to you. Most of the hands you are dealt are not worth playing. They will cost you a great deal of money in the long run if you don't exercise the discipline to throw them away.

It's not glamorous. It's not memorable, but it *is* poker's

basic bread-and-butter play. We fold most of the time. Even loose players probably fold more than they call, and even the most unrepentant maniacs might fold more often than they raise. Face it; good, solid, selective-and-aggressive players fold most of the time. But it doesn't come across in the literature that way. While we're used to reading about those big confrontations upon which reputations are made and myths are created, there's generally a lot of down time between watershed events. And most of that downtime is the result of looking at your cards, deciding that they are plug ugly and not worth a plug nickel's investment. So throw them away.

It's high time we created a better appreciation for the unglamorous act of laying your hand down, avoiding the fray for the time being, and saving your money for a better situation.

Do You Fold Often Enough?

The single biggest mistake made by most poker players is that they call when they should have folded. After all, most recreational players come to play—not to lay down their hands—and many get involved in pots with weak, unplayable starting hands. There are hold'em players who will see the flop with any ace in their hand, regardless of their position in the betting order, with no consideration for the number of opponents in the pot, or the amount of betting and raising that has taken place before it is their turn to act.

Folding in Split-Pot Games

The problem with calling far too often, when folding would be the better course of action, is not limited to hold'em either.

It is an epidemic in Omaha/8. With four cards in their hand, many players just can't resist seeing the flop. The sad truth is that the more potential starting hand combinations you're dealt—and with four cards dealt to you in Omaha you have six unique two-card combinations, compared to just one in hold'em—the more selective you should be.

In other words, you should play fewer Omaha/8 hands than hold'em hands. But that's just the reverse of what many players do. When they play Omaha/8, they frequently fall in love with every hand they're dealt.

Those Omaha/8 cards need to be coordinated to give you a reasonably good shot at winning. A hand like A♥-A♦2♣3♦ is an incredibly well-coordinated hand, with two potential nut flush draws, a low draw with counterfeit protection, and a big pair that might get better. Compare that hand to something like K♠J♣5♦5♥. Two big cards and a small pair is a treacherous hand. Make a set of fives and you've put at least one low card on board to give anyone with a low draw hope of chopping your pot in half. Your two high cards are not suited, and while you could make a straight with them, straight possibilities look a lot better when the cards all work together. When a hold'em player sits down to play Omaha, they often can't bear the thought of throwing away two kings pre-flop, much less two pairs—especially if they're in a low-limit game. Yet that is what they should do with this hand.

We see 7-stud/8 players who enter pots with an eight as their door card, that is, the card that is visibly open, even when their opponents show lower cards. Let's face it, in a split-pot game like 7-stud/8, if someone has an ace showing, you have no idea whether he's hoping to make a high hand, a low one, or is hoping to scoop. Suffice to say, if you've got an eight as your door card and an opponent is showing an ace, he probably has a better high *and* a better low hand than you do, assuming he has two other low cards snuggled in under that ace.

Draw to the Best Hand

Most of the time you should be drawing to the best possible low hand, otherwise the cost of making the second-best hand can become prohibitively expensive. While there are exceptional situations, where you don't have to have the best low draw to keep playing, they come up infrequently.

If you have a low draw along with a flush draw, you certainly don't need the best low draw to keep playing. Two-way hands—and that includes two-way draws—have a lot of playability because of the possibilities of scooping. After all, you might catch a low card of the suit you're chasing and make a flushy-low. Most of the time, a flush is good enough to win the high side, and whenever that's the case, your quest for a low hand amounts to a free roll. But you usually won't have that potent a draw, and if you're uncertain whether you'll wind up with the best hand, if you catch the cards you need, think about folding instead of calling.

Mirror, Mirror on the Wall: Should I Call? Should I Call?

Calling, in fact, is often the worst of the three alternatives of folding, raising, or calling. After all, if you've got a winning low hand, but it's one that looks like it might be a high hand, too—perhaps your board is scary enough to suggest a straight or flush, but all you really have is a good low with one pair—you ought to be raising. If you can drop a better high hand, you just might scoop the pot instead of splitting it. So don't lose sight of your objective in split-pot games: Scoop the pot whenever possible. Far too many players call as their default action. Instead, they ought to think first of folding or raising, and call as a last resort rather than a first option.

Folding in Hold'em

In hold'em you frequently see players who call with hands they should have folded. This is particularly true when players cold-call a raise. You need a much stronger hand to call a raise than you do to raise the pot yourself. After all, calling a raise requires a hand that figures to be better than the one held by the player doing the raising. The reason we've emphasized this point throughout the book is that it is so critical to one's success. And as true as it is for fixed-limit cash games—the kind you're most likely to find at your local casino—it's more true for pot-limit and no-limit cash games, and for tournament poker, too.

You'll often be dealt a hand that you are preparing to raise with, only to have an opponent snatch the rug right out from under your feet by raising before the action gets around to you. Most of the time, this is no longer even a calling hand, and it should wind up in the muck. When the initiative is filched from right under their noses, many players become irritated. You see it all the time, an angry slam-down of a hand like A-T because a player raised before they could act.

These players are wearing their emotions inside out. Instead of being upset, they ought to be thankful. Their opponent's raise probably saved them money, and they should be relieved, not angry. After all, money saved is just as spendable as money won, and any time you can get a free pass out of a pot, knowing your hand is probably a long shot that won't be offset by the pot odds, you should be a happy camper.

When faced with a raise, the hand you're holding quickly changes categories: Most likely it becomes either a folding hand or one you should reraise with; it's seldom a calling hand. If you're in the cutoff seat—the seat that acts immediately prior to the button—or on the button, and someone raises before it's your turn to act, you should throw away hands like A-J or A-T. Do this even if you would have raised with those same hands had no one entered the pot before the action reached you. On the other hand, if you're holding a big pair or A-K, you should make it three bets in hopes of playing heads up against the initial raiser. When that happens you have a big advantage going into the flop. Not only did you get the last raise in, you also have position on your opponent throughout the entire hand.

That doesn't mean you are obligated to play that hand down to the river. If you made it three bets with Q-Q and the flop contained an ace and a king, continuing to play if there was any appreciable action would be foolish. But if no overcards fall, you're a favorite over anyone who would raise with a pair of nines through a pair of aces, as well as A-K, A-Q, A-J, and K-Q.

Later Folds

The longer you're involved in a hand, the more difficult it becomes to fold. Often the size of the pot has grown big enough to make drawing correct, even when your chances of winning might be pretty slim. The opposite can be true, too. If you've flopped a straight draw against only one opponent in a hold'em game, chances are you will not be getting the right odds to keep calling.

Sometimes you'll find out via the betting and raising that you are not the favorite, even when you hold what ordinarily is a good hand. You might have been the aggressor before the flop with A–K or been fortunate enough to see an ace hit the board, watching in shocked indignation when there's a bet, a call, and a raise before it's your turn to act. Top pair, even with top kicker, is probably no good any longer, particularly if the board contains three cards of the same suit, or an obvious straight draw. Even if there's no flush possible, one of your opponents might have made a set and is now a prohibitive favorite. You can keep calling—your opponents will love you for it if you do—or you can do the smart thing and save your money for a better opportunity.

Sometimes you'll find situations that are easy folds; other times they are strictly judgment calls. These are based on how well you read your opponents and your analysis of the betting and raising that has transpired before the action reaches you. Experience helps. So does your willingness to see things as they really are. Do not play poker with a denial mind-set that allows you to talk yourself into calling with top pair because some part of your brain wants to believe that your opponent really did not make a flush.

When the Pot Grows Large

Sometimes the pot grows so big that even when most of the signals suggest you are beaten, you will wind up calling one last bet on the river. It happens. Although calling when you should have folded and folding when you should have called are both errors, it's a lot more catastrophic to fold the winning hand (and lose the entire pot in the process) than it is to call with the worst hand and lose one additional bet. If you fold a hand that would have won, you might lose ten or twelve bets. If you win at the rate of one big bet per hour, it can take you an entire day, or longer, to overcome that mistake.

2

TACTICS, STRATEGIES, AND PLOYS

This is where poker's rubber meets the road. Without strategy, tactics, and a few tricks up your sleeve, all the conceptual knowledge, mathematics, and theory won't do you any good. It's time to put them to play in your game. The tactics, strategies, and ploys that follow are what you can extract from your poker toolbox and employ when the situation warrants. If some of these tactics are new to you, then we'll have opened your eyes to new weaponry at your disposal. If they're already familiar to you, we hope you'll make even better use of them. Not only will these ploys and plays work for you, using them will lend an element of deception to the rest of your game, too.

A Common Strategy Against a Newbie or "Fish" Is Simply to Call with Any Two Cards and Then Outplay Them

This strategy presupposes that the newbie will call far too often before the flop. Then he'll show a willingness to toss his hand away if the flop does not help him. If that's his style, you can play aggressively whenever your opponent displays a passive attitude toward the pot. Your bet is likely to take it, even if you are on a stone-cold bluff. Some newbies will play just like we've described, and they do so because they are new to the game, unsure about what the proper cause of action should be. They're reluctant to look foolish by calling with a weak hand and then having to show it down at the hand's conclusion.

If you're new to the game, you can even make an obvious early bad call, so that your opponents will peg you for a weak player. When that happens, you've opened the door to myriad opportunities to outfox your opponents, each of whom thinks he has a pretty good line on your play. But be careful not to go too far with this. If you play too many hands and are viewed as a fish by too many players, more people will try to beat you. It will be harder to win hands against so many opponents. When too many players are in every hand, the chances increase that someone else will either have a better hand or develop a hand that will beat yours. If this happens, you need to be extra vigilant about getting proper pot odds to take down just the largest pots and leave the little ones for the true fish. This can all be encapsulated in a few short words of advice: Be the one who folds the most; it's a profitable way to play.

If you're the informed newcomer who can sense when an expert has called you just to outplay you, turn the tables on them and outplay them! When your hand hits and they're on your left, the best play you can make is to trap them. Check and call until the fish has reeled in the fisherman and then check/raise! Get such experts to call your extra bet on the river and take down a huge pot. If you're a good player who is roundly underestimated, you can take advantage of every single player who comes after you. Now that's a seafood dinner!

Free Card Raise

If you raise to get a free card on a more expensive betting round, then take the free card! And later you can use the same move as a bluff. Raise on a flush draw. Check the turn and bet on the river when the flush hits. Here's an example of the free card play. You're in late position and call with T♠9♠ after two opponents limp in to the pot. Your opponent bets when J♠9♣4♠ flops. To make the free card play, you'll need to raise, even though your hand does not figure to be the best one right now, especially if you know your opponent usually plays big cards such as K-J, Q-J, or A-J. Unless he's flopped at least two pair, he can't really be sure he has the best hand at this point either, so he'll probably check to the raiser when the turn card is dealt.

If the turn card is to your liking, go ahead and bet. If it's not, and everyone checks, go ahead and check behind them. By doing this, you've spent an additional small bet on the flop and saved a big bet on the turn. The result: A small bet saved (if the turn card is not one you were hoping for) and an additional half bet gained from each opponent (if the turn brought the card that completes your hand). You may get a chance to bet the river if your card comes. If not, you can fold and you've gotten to the river for the cost of one small bet.

One error you see all the time in hold'em games is one made by good-but-not-great players. They'll set up the free card play just as we described, and then they'll come out betting the turn instead of taking the free card. We know what they're thinking. "If I don't bet, I can't knock my opponents out of the pot and win it." The problem is that a bet won't eliminate anyone with top pair, so betting second pair rather than taking the free card that's been offered, is simply going to cost an additional bet. In essence, you've done your opponent's work for him by helping the player with the best hand get more money into a pot he figures to win.

The free card play is sort of a heads you win, tails they lose situation. It's one you should make good use of whenever the opportunity presents itself, and making good use of it includes taking the free card when it's offered to you.

Changing Speeds

Regardless of your own individual playing style, you'll have to vary it to deceive skillful opponents who begin reading you like an open book. It's important to realize that changing speeds is not necessary against opponents who are unobservant. They would never even notice that you're playing differently now than you were a few minutes ago. In fact, they seldom notice anything but their own cards, and they tend to play them without regard for their opponent's playing style or cards anyway.

Against good players, you can be sure that they have clocked you and are building a "book" on your playing style. Once your savvier opponents know your playing tendencies, you can make money by playing out of character. If they see you as a very conservative player, the kind who seldom bluffs, you have earned a license to steal. Now you have a free ticket to bet into a big pot and not get called, unless your opponent also has a very good hand, one that she's willing to risk a significant amount of money on in a confrontation with a player she knows only bets with the goods.

If you're seen as a very aggressive player, just keep betting your big hands. You can count on being called by any number of observant players who are convinced that you're trying to steal the pot out from under their noses once again.

What happens when you're involved in a hand with skilled players, as well as those who will keep on calling until the bitter end? That's sometimes referred to as a *protected pot*, and the stubborn players you can never drive off the pot are precluding you from using any sophisticated plays on your skilled opponents, or even trying a routine, run-of-the-mill bluff.

For any tactical ploy to be successful, it has to work against all your opponents and not just one of them. It does no good to successfully drive a better player out of the pot if you can't pry out the calling stations, too. So in situations such as these, you're forced to play fairly straightforward poker, and you'll generally have to show down the best hand to win the pot. That's okay, because your sophisticated opponents realize that, too. They'll also know that fancy plays in pots where at least one opponent will call them, all the way and all the time, are usually costly and doomed to fail.

Dealing with Your Own Default Programming

This is easier said than done. All of us have default programming hard wired into our poker style that gets us playing in certain predictable patterns. To deviate from that style, we must consciously make up our minds to get out of our usual modes and start playing differently.

As in all facets of life, we often have to leave our comfort zone to be successful. And there's an art to determining when to make the switch. After all, if you're playing good hands and your opponents are calling most of the time, there's no need to change styles in order to run a bluff or two. In fact, if you are being called, your bluffs are very likely to fail.

If you're able to steal pots with an overly aggressive

style against opponents who are unwilling to pull the trigger and call you, you ought to keep it up until they finally muster up the courage to start firing back at you. Only when you feel that it's time to duck and cover should you then switch styles, tighten up, and hope to get called on your very good hands.

You just can't expect to have as much success playing at the polar extremes of style (i.e., overly tight or overly aggressive) as you can if you mix up your play by varying your strategy. But do so in a manner that zigs when your opponent is prepared to think you just zagged. If this sounds like mom's "all things in moderation" mantra, you're right. For the most part, it is. But where it differs lies in your ability to paint a picture of your playing style that your opponents will buy, and then snatching away some of their money by playing differently.

If You're Thinking About Playing a Hand, Think About Raising

We all have default positions, and when we're playing poker many of us have programmed ourselves to call, rather than raise or fold. Calling is frequently the default course of action when we're trying to decide what to do with the hand we've been dealt. But if no one else has entered the pot when the action gets around to you, instead of thinking about calling—which is passive play at best—raising or folding is probably the best way to go.

Limping Can Be Like Painting a "Hit Me with Your Best Shot" Sign on Your Back

Limping—when you're not trapping—invites others into the pot with you and those players are in better position behind you. It also invites them to raise in order to seize control of every betting round. If you've called with a mediocre hand, the kind that would have been better off consigned to the discard pile, you've created the added burden of having to act before the player who raised you. If you have a middling hand and she did raise, perhaps she is doing so on a stone-cold bluff. She also could really have a superior hand. If she does, you're looking at finessing a very narrow path of cards in order to to win this pot.

And let's face it, hope is not the way to win at poker. In fact, hope is the death of many poker players because the truth of the matter is that better starting hands wind up winning the majority of the time. Hopeful hands are usually crushed in the process.

If you decided to raise when you entered the pot, the guy who acted after you will probably not bluff and release his hand. By raising, when you're the first player to enter the pot, you've taken control of the hand. Now your opponent is the one who has to make a decision: *Are you bluffing or do you have a real hand?* Regardless of what his decision is, he's going to be wrong some of the time. By allowing him to make mistakes in judgment, you've increased your potential for winning.

Choosing Your Raising Hands

What should you raise with? If you're first to act, you don't want to play hands that figure to do well only with a whole gaggle of opponents. A hand like 9-8 suited, which could grow into a very big hand such as a straight or flush, just isn't the kind of hand you want to play in a heads-up situation. After all, if you don't flop a flush or straight or even a good draw, all you're left with is 9-high, and that's not going to win very many pots. In these situations, you're much better off playing big cards or pairs and tossing away anything else you might have been dealt.

Raising on the Button

If you're on the button and no one else has entered the pot, you can raise with a wide variety of hands. Any pair will do, or even a single big card in your hand. But be forewarned. When you come out raising and no one else has entered the pot, it smells of a bluff. You'll be called by anyone with even a fair hand, and you might find yourself reraised by an opponent who wants to take the initiative and tempo away from you.

If you're raising from the button with a pair of deuces, or a pair of sixes, you have to be prepared to continue betting regardless of the flop. By doing this, you're putting pressure on your opponent. Now he has to at least stop and consider if you are still bluffing or actually have a big hand. If you bet the flop, you almost always have to fire another salvo on the turn, too, unless the board is threatening because three cards of one suit are present, or it's sequenced with cards in the playing zone. A flop of J-T-9-6 is a good example of that. It's not all peaches and cream when you raise from the button. It's a raise from what's called *steal position*, and even if you're not stealing, it looks for all the world as though you are.

The flip side of this coin is that when you are dealt a good hand on the button, and come out raising, many of your opponents won't believe you. They'll think you're doing what they, and almost every other player would do, and that's bet if you're on the button because no one has acted yet.

If you can't decide whether to come in for a raise or fold, we'd recommend erring on the side of caution and releasing your hand. It's usually less expensive that way.

Raising Considerations in Pot-Limit and No-Limit Games

If all of the above is true for limit poker, it's doubly true if you're playing pot-limit or no-limit poker. Pots in these games can grow incredibly large in the wink of an eye. You really don't want to call and give your opponent an opportunity to come in for one measly little bet along with the chance of flopping a miraculous hand that will win an enormous pot for him.

If your opponent wants a chance to stick around and try to flop a big hand, you have to charge him dearly for it. That's not to say you should overbet the pot—three or four times the big blind is a betting standard that many no-limit players use. If he comes over the top and reraises you, you'll be forced to decide whether he's bluffing, or whether he has picked up a big pocket pair such as K-K or A-A.

That's not going to happen all that often. Most players simply don't reraise as a bluff in a no-limit game. That's because if their opponent really does have the goods, he figures to win a big, big pot. So the structure and potential for huge pots serves as somewhat of a damper on many pot- and no-limit games.

If you raise pre-flop, it's like having four cards. You get to play the cards you have plus the ones you represent.

When to Raise Other Callers, and When Calling Is a Better Idea

While you can—in fact, you should—raise the blinds when you are first to enter a pot from middle or late position and have any reasonably strong hand, if there are a few callers already in the pot when it's your turn to act, you'll need a bigger hand to raise than you would if you were first to act. And you'll need a bigger hand than that if you intend to cold-call a raise for two or more bets.

Just how big a hand you need will depend on your opponents. If they are all very tight players who seldom bluff and usually have the goods when they enter a pot, you can take it for a given that at least one of them, and probably more, have pretty good hands. If you have a pretty good hand, too—perhaps a middle pair such as 8-8, or a big-card hand such as A-T or A-J, you'll have to decide whether your opponents would call with lesser hands. Or if they would raise from their position if they had the same hand you did.

The object of this analysis is to determine how you think your hand stacks up in relation to the opposition. If you've got a better hand, you might consider raising instead of calling, especially if a raise will dissuade players who act after you from entering the pot, too. After all, it's one thing for a caller in late position to take a flyer by calling with a hand such as 8–7, especially if a number of players have already entered the pot for one bet. It's another thing entirely to cold-call a raise when your hand no longer figures to be anywhere near the best. You're faced with swimming upstream in an expensive pot with fewer callers than you need to compensate for the long odds against making the best hand.

Flexible Thinking Based on Your Opponents' Actions

What's at work here is more psychological than it is anything else. After all, we love to play, to get involved, and to mix it up in pots when we have good hands. But poker is relative. And if you were sitting there thinking you were dealt a playable hand prior to any action taking place, it can be difficult to reassess your hand. This is because of the action that transpired in the moments between first viewing the hand and your turn to fold, call, raise, or reraise. Sometimes a hand you were mentally prepared to play becomes a folding hand. Regardless of your first thoughts when you looked at your two starting cards, you'll need to come to terms with the realization that poker is a game of relative values, and your hand must now be released.

On the other hand, when there are already callers active in the pot, certain hands that you might have been preparing to release, such as 8–7 or a small pair, now become playable. The reason for this is because of the multitude of callers, coupled with the fact that you can see the pot for one bet and one bet only. This gives you a chance to take a shot at a pot offering huge implied odds if you get lucky. This opportunity arises as a direct consequence of all those additional players in the pot—some of them will presumably stick around to pay you off if you flop a set, a straight, or a draw to a straight that you are able to complete on a later betting round.

What's happening here is that the size of the pot and the low cost of getting involved makes it correct to play hands that do well against several players. Medium-sized pairs such as 5-5, 6-6, 7-7, 8-8, and 9-9 and suited connectors such as T-9 are examples of these hands.

While we usually advise aggressive play as a key to winning poker, it's important to play selectively, too. And hands like these simply don't fare very well against few opponents because they usually need to improve to win. Needing improvement is a phrase that translates into a drawing hand, one that needs to be hit by the flop at least once, and possibly twice, in order to grow into the best hand. That means you need a few opponents who will build the pot to a size that offsets the odds against making the best hand. Calling is the right choice in these situations.

You're in a delicate place. Your hand is not strong enough to raise with. In fact, it does not figure to be the best hand right now. However, the pot odds are big enough to offset the longish odds against making your hand, and so folding would be incorrect, too. You're left with calling as the best, if not the only, course of action.

When You Have a Big Hand and Someone Raises

If you've been dealt a very big hand, a pair of queens or higher—or perhaps A-K, depending on the kinds of hands you think the raiser might have—you need to carry selective and aggressive play to a newer and higher level. Now you're faced with calling two bets cold. No longer are those K-Js playable if you're fairly certain your opponent raised with a hand that's bigger and better than that. Now you have to choose: Either step deftly out of the way by folding or making it three bets to go by reraising. If you have a big hand, yours might not be the best right now. But even if your opponent had a hand that is better than yours, you might get lucky on the flop. Your aggressive reraise might also allow you to seize the initiative on the flop. If that happens, you can either bet, if you think you have the best hand or believe a wager might cause your opponent to fold, or you can check after your opponent does and take a free card.

If you call in a situation like this, it's usually because you have a good but not great hand. If you have a powerful hand, such as K-K or A-A, there's not much mystery here. You've probably got the best hand so reraising is the easy and best decision. But if you have a so-so hand, one that you'd probably have called with if the pot had not been raised, you are going to be better off releasing that hand under most circumstances. When you need to have the flop hit you twice in order to be competitive in the hand, you are a decided long shot. You're just looking for trouble if you call instead of releasing your hand.

If a solid player raises and you're sitting there with A-J, A-T or K-Q—hands that look good under most circumstances—you are better off folding. This is because your opponent probably has a hand that's better than yours. The raiser probably has either a pair of tens or higher, or two high cards that include an ace. If he has the latter, he probably has A-K or A-Q and any ace you have with a lesser kicker is likely to be dominated, leaving you with only three outs. That's never a pretty picture. If he has a pair, your two big cards are only small underdogs against a pair of eights, nines, and tens, but a decided underdog against J-J, Q-Q, K-K, or A-A.

Look at the situation realistically. You're a small favorite—many players call it a coin flip—against some of your opponents' likely hands, a big underdog against others, and dominated to three outs against still others. Overall, you figure to lose a lot of money on these kinds of confrontations in the long run.

Pocket Jacks Are a Dilemma

If you're holding a pair of queens, kings, or aces, or A-K, you can go ahead and reraise. But you're better off folding all other hands when facing a raise. If you're holding a pair of jacks, you've got a hand on the cusp. The flop figures to contain a card bigger than a jack about half the time. Even if you have the best hand right now, a pair of jacks is vulnerable against a raise. In a no-limit game or in a tournament, you're really rolling the dice when confronting a raise with a pair of jacks. Of course, if you're short stacked and facing elimination in short order anyway, making a stand with a pair of jacks is probably the best thing you can do. That pair of jacks figures to be the best hand you'll be dealt before you're forced to play a couple of random cards from one of the blinds. At that point in a tournament, you have run almost completely out of options. You can't sit around and wait for a better hand; you're not likely to be dealt a bigger one in the near future. You can't bluff with a lesser hand because your short stack size means someone is likely to call you regardless of their holdings. When your back is to the wall, and you're completely out of running room, you have no choice. Push all your chips into the center of the table and hope.

Hope, as we've pointed out earlier in this book, spells the death of many poker players. In this case, you've no other options available to you. When you enter a poker room, you may want to heed the words of Danté's *The Divine Comedy*, written 700 years ago: "All hope abandon, ye who enter here."

If the Raiser Is on the Button, Is He Trying to Steal the Pot?

There's one other caveat. When you have a late position player opening the pot for a raise, you have to think about whether he is doing so with a weak hand in an attempt to steal the blinds. How can you determine whether he has the goods or not? The best way is to know your opponents. Some will rarely raise without a good hand or two big cards. Others will raise with any two cards from late position if the pot has not been opened by the time it's their turn to act.

When you are facing a player who might be raising on a

bluff, you can open up your playing repertoire a bit and reraise. By making it three bets to go, you will almost certainly knock out all but the most stubborn opponents. You are also playing what's probably the best hand against one opponent and some dead money from the blinds in the pot. Moreover, your third bet will allow you to seize the initiative and take control of the pot by betting the flop and the turn.

Blind Ambition

Many players are unsure about how to play their blinds. When you're in early position, you're at a big disadvantage because you have to act first. When you act first, you don't have any idea about the real or purported strength of anyone else's hands. Unless you can pick up some strong visual clues about what your opponents might do when it's their turn to act, you are truly flying blind.

As a result, early to act means greater selectivity about the hands you choose to play. Although the blinds do have the advantage of seeing everyone else act first before the flop, this small edge is more than offset because they are forced to wager money without regard to the strength of their hands. They will also have the disadvantage of having to act first on each succeeding round of betting.

The small blind is in a worse position than the big blind. The big blind can frequently call raises with mediocre hands because it will only cost him one small bet to do so. In effect he is getting better odds to make this call. The small blind cannot be as free with his money. His cost to call a raise is higher, and that reduces the odds he is offered by the pot.

Blind Odds

Here's how it works: If anyone other than the small blind raises, the big blind will get a minimum of 3.5-to-1 to call. This is because there will be one small bet that he posted, two small bets from the raiser, and one-half of a small bet from the small blind. If there are more players involved in the hand, then the big blind will be offered even greater odds.

But the small blind has to act before the big blind and will be required to invest an additional 1.5 small bets to call the initial raise. He also has to do so without knowing what the big blind will do. If the big blind folds, then the small blind has odds of 3.5-to-1.5, or 2.3-to-1. These odds are not nearly as good as those given to the big blind. If the big blinds calls after the small blind, then the small blind will have gotten odds of 3-to-1. While that might not seem much worse than the big blind's odds, consider this: by calling, the small blind guarantees that the big blind receives odds of 5-to-1 to see the flop.

What does all this mean in the heat of battle? Even if you are not prone to work out the pot odds, bear in mind that you need to have a much stronger hand to call a raise from the small blind than you do when you're the big blind. It's all a question of value for money, and the big blind gets a better price to see flops than the small blind does.

Check-Raising from the Blind

When you are in the blind, you have very few strategic options at your disposal. Check-raising is probably the most effective tactical ploy you can bring to bear against aggressive opponents who will bet whenever you check. Employ this strategy whenever you think you have the best hand or you want to get more money into the pot. Against more passive opponents, you can take the opposite tack and bet into them. But take heed: You may have to fire twice in order to get results. If you bet and are called, unless you want to give up your bluff and probably surrender the pot, you have to be prepared to come out betting the turn, and quite possibly the river, too.

Stealing Blinds

If you're in one of the later positions and everyone has folded, don't ever call. Decide instead whether to fold or to raise. There's no formula you can follow to come up with the right decision. Consider these factors when deciding which road to choose:

- While you can never know for sure what your opponents in the blinds were dealt, any ace figures to be good. Any king stands a good chance of being the best hand, too. A pair is a monster against two random cards, but smallish suited connectors, such as 7♠6♠, which may look good against a big field for one bet, are decided dogs in a short-handed situation. Short handed, the edge goes to the big cards, and it stays with the big cards regardless of the smaller card configurations. For example, A♥K♦ is a 67–33 percent favorite against 8♣3♠, and the latter is a hand no one ever gets excited about. But against 8♣7♣, one of those tony suited connectors that many players adore, A♥K♦ is still a 58–42 percent favorite. While it's not quite the favorite that it is against the trashy 8-3, it's still a big favorite and neither the factor that 8-7 is both suited, as well as connected, lends that much more value to the hand.

- Some players never relinquish their blinds. Well, almost never. Against players like this, you have very little bluffing equity, and you'll have to bet your hand for value if you decide to come in for a raise. Nevertheless, heads-up, any hand containing an ace is one that can be bet for value, since it figures to be the best hand right now. Even though loose players—the kind who defend their blinds too frequently—are impossible to bluff, they give up so much equity through poor play that betting even otherwise mediocre hands for value has merit against them.

- Are your adversaries tricky and aggressive? Aggressive, sophisticated players may well realize that you don't need much of an edge to raise their blinds from late position. They also might be aggressive enough to risk a reraise, based on the assumption that you are probably raising with a less-than-premium hand. While your opponent in the blind has no idea whether you're holding A-A or A-4, he's predicating his reraise on the fact that you are more likely to be raising with a lone ace in your hand than with a pair of them. If the tricky, aggressive player is in the small blind, he knows that by reraising he may be able to drop the big blind and possibly get you to release your hand if you had raised with a weak holding. If you peg your opponents as tough, tricky, and aggressive—fully capable of playing back at you—you should try to steal the blind with your good hands, not your marginal holdings.

- Predictable opponents are easy to play against;

tough, tricky ones are not. When your predictable opponent check-raises, you are beaten. When that tough, tricky opponent check-raises, you are in a guessing game of sorts, and you will seldom be sure of the correct line of play to pursue. Even if your opponent is not especially tricky, but simply plays well, attempted steals have less equity. This is because good opponents will get out of the way with their lesser hands, play back at you with their good ones, and bluff with just about the right frequency to defeat any attempts on your part to react to them.

- If you haven't attempted to steal the blinds since the Carter administration, your opponents are more likely to give you credit for a good hand and fold to your raise. On the other hand, if you've raised quite a bit lately—and it doesn't matter one whit whether those raises were because you were dealt a spate of hands like A-A, K-K, or Q-Q or you were robbing them blind with 3-2, 7-2, and 9-3—any time your opponents think you may be taking advantage of them, they are more likely to call or even to reraise. No one likes to be bullied, especially poker players. Eventually even the most timid of opponents will straighten up and take a stand. The message here is clear. If you've done a lot of blind stealing lately, slow down and save your raises for really good hands; then hope they decide to stand up and call you.

Defending Your Blinds

This is the opposite side of the coin. When you're the one facing a raise from a late position player who's first to enter the pot, you have to decide whether to fold, call (and hope for the best on the flop) or play back at him by reraising. When you're in this position, here's what you need to consider:

- If you have the best hand, consider reraising. If you're in the small blind, this is a particularly good idea because you can force the big blind to commit two bets to the pot in order to continue playing. If you can eliminate the big blind, you accomplish two objectives: You get to play the pot heads up against the raiser, who may not have much of a hand at all. And you've succeeded in getting some dead money in the pot. Raising from the big blind forces your opponents to put more money into the pot, too. But, as long as it's only one additional bet, he'll call your raise every time. As a practical matter, the edge you gain is that if the blind thief has a weak hand, he's likely to fold to a bet on the flop. Although he correctly called your raise because the price was right, your aggression will probably convince him to release his hand if the flop does not fit.
- If your opponent habitually raises in these situations, you won't need much of a reason or much of a hand to play back at him. But if he seldom practices this kind of larceny, you can probably credit him with a hand and release all but the best of yours.
- If your adversary is a good player, you will be confronting him for the remainder of the hand out of position. You will have to act first, and if you check, he'll probably bet. If you bet, he's likely to raise. But you won't know what he's going to do with

any degree of certainty and it precludes you from any really deceptive, tricky maneuvers as a consequence. On the other hand, if you can outplay your opponent, you can use that skill to negate his positional advantage. But please don't make the mistake of underestimating opponents. While we all like to think we can outplay the opposition, having a positional disadvantage is like a horse giving up weight in a race. It tends to equalize differences at best, while at worst the positional advantage your seemingly pedestrian opponent has may be just enough to tip the scales in his favor.

Betting When the Wrong Draw Hits

Sometimes you can steal the pot when you have a drawing hand but the wrong draw appears to come in. Suppose you have 8♦7♦ and the flop is 9♠6♠2♣. You have four cards to a straight, but no hope of making a flush. But suppose you come out betting when another spade hits the board. If your opponent doesn't suspect you of bluffing, you have a good chance to represent a flush. Even if you are called, you still have outs to a straight on the river. One disadvantage to this play can occur if you bet and your opponent raises, representing a flush. Now you've got a decision to make, and it's not an easy one. Another troubling scenario is when you bet the turn representing a flush and are called, and a fourth spade falls on the river. Even if that fourth spade gave you a straight, you cannot be aggressive under those circumstances. You may even have to release your hand.

Raising Out the Wrong Opponents

Sometimes you can be too aggressive for your own good. That usually happens when you have a draw that figures to win the pot if you connect, but lose if you miss. Suppose you have a flush draw against five opponents and one of them seems to have all the earmarks of a good hand. If the opponent who appears to have a good hand is to your right, and you decide to raise on a semi-bluff, you run the risk of eliminating anyone else who may call with a hand that figures to lose to yours if you make your flush.

In this case, raising will turn a multiple-player pot into one that's heads up. Since the chances of your raise knocking out the player with a good hand are small, semi-bluffing is not the right tactic for this situation. In this situation you want all the adversaries you can drag into the pot with you, so that you will be paid off handsomely if you make your flush. When you flop a flush draw, the odds against completing it by the river are only 1.86–to–1. And the more players you have in the pot with you to pay you off when fortune smiles, the better you'll like it.

However, if the player with the good hand is seated to your immediate left—or at least on that side of the table—and he comes out betting, you should raise to trap all those opponents who called for one bet in the midst of the pot. Now your raise figures to get a lot of money into the pot, more than enough to offset those 1.86-to-1 odds against completing your hand.

How Often Do You Bluff; How Often Should You Bluff?

Many players wonder how often they should bluff. They worry whether they're bluffing too often or not bluffing enough. From the casual conversations you overhear in poker rooms, some players seem to obsess about this. It's almost as if there is some optimal bluffing frequency that they should know about but don't. They wonder whether savvier opponents have tuned into some strategy. They feel they're missing the boat.

The simple answer is that there really is no optimum frequency. If you're bluffing 8 percent of the time, or 10, or 12, it's not really information that makes a difference in understanding how you're doing as a bluffer. What does matter is *when you bluff*, and *who you bluff*. Those two are related concepts.

If you bluff at the wrong time or you attempt to bluff players who never fold—unless their hands are absolutely hopeless and there are no cards to come—your bluffing will go to waste. And it doesn't matter whether you bluff 8, 10, or 12 percent of the time. If you bluff at the wrong time, and you attempt to bluff the wrong players, it all goes for naught.

Instead of looking for some abstract number as a guide to the portion of time you should be bluffing, look at your results instead. But even this is tricky. Here's why.

If Your Bluffs Are Seldom Called

If your bluffs are never called, that's not as good as you might think at first. Of course it means you're winning each and every time you bluff, but it also means you are probably not bluffing enough. After all, if your bluffs are called only one time in four and you bluffed three times today and won each of those pots, imagine what would happen if you had bluffed eight times.

Twice you would have been called. You would have lost one additional bet, for a total of two units over and above what you would have lost had you checked the river and lost to your opponent in a showdown. But on six of those occasions you would have won the pot. And if we assume that each pot averaged six units, you would have a net win of thirty-four units (6 winning bluffs x 6 units per pot = 36 units, minus 2 additional units lost when you bluffed, were called, and lost). Instead, you had a perfect bluffing record, but you only bluffed three times for a total of eighteen units (3 successful bluffs x 6 units per pot). The additional bluffing you did not carry out meant you left money on the table.

If this were the case, it means you are missing out on bluffing opportunities. Naturally, the more you bluff, the more you run the risk of opponents calling you. Even so, you don't have to win each and every time you bluff to be successful. You just have to find some optimal bluffing frequency that allows you to rake in all the additional chips you might currently be missing out on, while not bluffing so often that you are seen as an inveterate bluffer.

If this happens, or it seems like it's about to happen—or even if you notice that you're called more often than you were before you began to bluff a bit more—you can change strategies and bet for value whenever you have a hand that you think is better than your opponent's. When opponents suspect you're bluffing too often, you stand more of a chance of winning an additional bet when betting for value.

Inducing Bluffs

If your opponents are prone to come out betting any time you show the slightest sign of weakness by checking, you have a perfect opportunity to induce a bluff on their part.

If you are first to act on the river, you can check. If your opponent is aggressive, he'll probably bet in an attempt to take the pot away from you. This is a terrific play when you suspect your opponent is on a draw to a straight or a flush, but would fold if you were to bet into him when he failed to complete his hand.

If he misses his draw, but you call when he bluffs at the pot, you gain a bet in the process. Presumably he would fold if you saw that his flush draw failed to materialize and you bet into him.

If he has a big, hidden hand—perhaps he called all the way with a pair smaller than yours and made a set on the river—you will save a bet. If you had come out betting, he would have raised and you would have to make a crying call on the river. It's a no-lose situation. You win an extra bet if you can induce him to bet on a weak hand. You also save a bet if he catches a miracle card that gives him a hidden hand he is just itching to raise with.

When Checking and Calling Is Better Than Betting

While we endorse and advocate selective and aggressive play, sometimes checking and calling is a better choice than betting or raising. This is one of those occasions. Any time you have a relatively aggressive opponent and you are not sure what kind of hand you are confronting—a stronger hand, a worse hand, or a busted draw—checking and calling is the way to go. However, against players who call far too frequently but are not aggressive about betting and raising, you would probably be better off betting any hand for value whenever you suspect your opponent has very low calling standards.

When Less Is More

While big hands are pretty to look at, there are some occasions when less is most assuredly more. One instance is when you'd rather be out from under another player's dominating hand. Suppose no one has called the blind and you raised with two big cards. The big blind calls and the two of you see the flop, which is 8-4-3 of mixed suits. This doesn't look too threatening at all, so you bet only to find yourself check-raised by the big blind, and he's a player whose game you respect.

What do you suppose he might have? Well, he might have been lying in the weeds with a big pocket pair, but it's more likely he called your raise with a hand like A-8. You know that he realizes it's more likely you raised with two big cards than a big pair, and he's intent on punishing you for your aggression by raising with what he suspects is the best hand.

If you have a very big hand, he's in trouble. If all you have are big cards that weren't helped by the flop, he's in the lead and that figures to be the case more often than not. If you had your choice of big cards to play at this point and chose A-K, you'd be shortchanging yourself. There's a much bigger chance that you would be dominated by your opponent. You would also have fewer live outs than you would if you picked two smaller cards, as long as the two cards you selected were bigger than the cards on the board.

It's not very likely that your opponent is holding a hand like J-T, which means you have six live cards to give you a bigger pair than your opponent. On the other hand, if you had A-K and he was holding A-8, any ace that fell would give you the illusion that you were in the lead. But it would only be an illusion, and a costly one at that. In reality, your opponent would have two pair and put you in a world of hurt. Only the king is a safe card, but there are just three of those left in the deck, and your chances are looking grim. But a pair of jacks or a pair of tens will beat a pair of eights just as surely as a pair of aces does, and those lower ranks are free from potential domination by your opponent's hand. Sometimes hold'em can be a very counterintuitive game.

Truth or Dare

When a guy says to you, "Fold, I'll show you," half the time he'll show you the bluff! Double whammy! It'll feel like he stole your pot *and* hit you in the stomach. Don't listen to what you hear, just what you see. Know that people often speak opposite to the truth. A good poker player will tell you whatever will works to his own advantage. Bad players don't need to tell you what they have; it's obvious. It's worth noting that it's far more likely that a male player would lie about a hand before showing a bluff than a woman.

Show and Tell

When people show each other hands privately, they're usually showing good hands and not outrageous bluffs. Some really confident pros, however, might use the opportunity to show their hands as an audacious bluff. Beware.

Showing the Bluff

Some experts advise never showing a bluff to your opponents. Others use a mixed strategy. They will show a bluff when they feel it will unnerve an opponent, but they'll refrain from showing their hand on other occasions. Some players will never show down their good hands either, while others will sometimes show down their big hands. This tells an opponent, "Hey, I never bluff; when I bet I've got a good hand—just as big a hand as the one I'm showing you now."

In the 1997 World Series of Poker at the final table, Stu Ungar was in the lead but Ron Stanley was mounting a comeback and was closing in on Ungar. A big pot developed where Ungar made a huge bet and Stanley thought and thought. Finally he threw his hand away, convinced that Stu Ungar had him beaten, and in any event Stanley probably did not want to lose all the chips he had so patiently built up over the past forty minutes. So he folded his tent. As the pot was being pushed to Ungar, he casually flipped his hand over with an air of insouciance. While the cards were flipping back down to the table, Stanley could see that Ungar had a meaningless Q-T, a complete bluff. Had he called, Stanley would have vaulted into the lead. But Ungar's bluff-reveal so unnerved Stanley that he played himself out of the tournament a few hands later.

Re-Reraising

Some players reraise or check-raise as a ploy. You can tell because they do it often. Counter this bluff by re-reraising— even when you're on a bluff. An especially good time to do this is on the flop. This is the exception to "you can't bluff a bluffer." If you do this, you need to bet the turn strong. If you get called or raised on the turn, they're not bluffing or best case, they're on a draw.

3

IMAGE

In life—and often in poker, too—you've got to be able to walk the walk as proficiently as you talk the talk. In the long run, all the gold chains, Rolex watches, and assorted other bling won't make you a poker player any more than a scalpel will turn a tree surgeon into a brain surgeon. You've got to be able to play the game to win. But in the tactical play, image is sometimes all you've got at your disposal to win a pot. It may be all you have to give your opponent the false sense of comfort he needs to bet into your power-house hand.

Either they've misled themselves or you've misled them. No poker player would make the wrong move if he could see his opponents' hands. That's where misinformation and the seeds of disinformation come into play. Image, the same weapon that allows us to crash parties as though we were invited guests, allows us to walk our opponents down a primrose path to their own destruction.

Only the Chip Runner Knows for Sure

When you sit down at any game of poker, the first and eas-iest thing to do is to scrutinize each and every player. Do you happen to know whether any of them is tight or weak? Are they in the current hand and the next hand after that? Do they look like they are winning or losing? More specifically, how big are their current chip stacks relative to the table? The chip stack is often an indication of a player's current success, but not always. Some players buy significantly more chips than the game at hand requires. They may do this because they are extremely loose and want to weather the usually enormous swings without constantly rebuying. Or they may do it to pace themselves, buying in for their whole day's bankroll and planning never to rebuy. Or, more likely, they may do it to intimidate newcomers to the game and look like winners. It won't take long for you to assess the truth about such posturers. The truly good players practice the slow build. The loose players put chips—usually dead chips—into every pot. These chips are only serving to build someone else's bankroll and stand no chance of taking down the pot. Make a mental note every time someone rebuys chips at a cash game.

The Hands Are as Much a Window to the Poker Player's Soul as the Eyes—So Is the Adam's Apple

Poker players are fond of saying things like, "I knew what he had because I was able to look into his soul." If that sounds like something you might expect to hear from a fortuneteller or a palm reader, you're probably not too far off. This is because poker players often do have a unique ability to deign opponents' hands from a variety of non-verbal clues and cues, known collectively as *tells*.

Although poker players can't really look into someone's soul, their cues do come from more tangible aspects of an opponent's game and that usually means reading his hands and his neck. Players take great pains to hide their expressions, sometimes wearing sunglasses or even those awful cat's eye glasses that Greg Raymer wore to shield his eyes during the 2004 World Series of Poker. While most don't carry it to the extent that Greg did with his sunglasses, many players are fond of wearing ball caps with the brims pulled down, so their eyes—after all, they're the windows to the soul—are shaded and tough to read.

Hand Tells Are More Easily Read Than Others

A poker player's hands are naked and exposed for the entire table to behold. Many players' hands will tremble slightly when they have a good hand. That trembling is a purely involuntary action that can't readily be controlled. It's a good clue in determining whether an opponent's big bet means a big hand or a bad bluff.

There are other involuntary cues, too: Blood vessels in the neck or an Adam's apple will pulse. It's a lot easier to watch for trembling hands (which is usually a sign of a very strong hand, but not always; it may mean the player simply has a tremor he can't control). While many players are fond of hiding behind sunglasses, most poker players who look for tells are really looking at their opponent's hands and neck, not their eyes. That's why you'll see some pros, like Phil "the unabomber" Laak, covered completely in a hooded sweat shirt pulled forward beyond the dark sunglasses. Note that players who go to such lengths to hide are keenly aware of every aspect of the game and bent on using every trick to their advantage.

The pros all know that tells are highly individualized, too. Although there are tells that are generally true for the majority of players, each one needs to be vetted against a particular opponent's playing style. Even if you've picked up a player-specific tell, it's probably not valid all of the time. And because a player who comes out betting or raising tends to keep on betting or raising (like physics, where a body in motion tends to stay in motion and a body at rest tends to stay at rest), it can cost a lot of money to chase down a raiser only to find that your tell was either inaccurate or inoperative for some reason.

The Importance of Betting with Confidence

Betting with confidence is critical. This is because there's usually a large gap between the way you bet with a big hand and how you bet when you're bluffing or have a weak hand. Bet the same way each time and you won't give your opponent a read on whether you have a good hand or a marginal one. Every astute player is always on the lookout for tells, and the more you can do to keep from broadcasting them, the better off you are. It's not only hand motions that give players away; there are other tells, too, and the pros know them all.

Furtive Glances, Posture Changes, Stare-Downs, and Chip-Slams

A glance at your hand and then a glance toward your chips is usually an indication of a strong hand. So is a slightly trembling hand that reaches for chips. Many players will sit up straight in their seats when they have a good hand, a distinct difference from the kind of table slouch that many players affect when they don't have a hand worth playing. Amateurish bluffs often include the near slamming of chips into the betting area along with a stare-down worthy of a snarling boxer attempting to intimidate his opponent. Conversely, sometimes it is so, so obvious when someone has missed their draw on the river that their body language practically screams, "If you bet like you have something, I will certainly fold; go ahead and take it." If you find yourself facing such a player, go ahead and make that confident bet. It goes without saying that you shouldn't be the one screaming, "Take it!"

Adopt an Orphaned Pot Today

Sometimes neither you nor your opponent will make a hand. When both of you check and then he checks a second time, the pot has been orphaned. It is begging to be taken by the first aggressive bet! So, come out betting on the final round. Your opponent may suspect you of bluffing. Heck, he may know you're bluffing. But without either a strong hand or the guts to raise you on a stone-cold bluff, he will be hard pressed to call. Yes, some of the time he will check, call, and beat you. At other times you will become sadly aware of the fact that you were set up by a player holding a monster hand. Most of the time, however, you'll see a pot that looks to have been abandoned. That's precisely what happened. If that pot is looking to be taken by the first player to risk a few chips, go ahead and do just that. Bet regardless of the hand you're holding and watch your opponent fold. You know you were bluffing; they probably do, too. But that's not important at all. What matters is that when a pot looks to have been abandoned, it usually is. And all you have to do is take it.

Miracles Happen

If you stay in for a miracle and you hit your miracle—bet it! In fact, any time you make the hand you were building toward, you should bet. If you can't or won't bet the hand you were hoping to make, why were you playing those

cards in the first place? It makes absolutely no sense whatsoever to play a hand you can't bet. If you play this way,
you'll win the minimum on hands that capture the pot.
But you're likely to *lose* the maximum on hands that are
not completed. This is because the vast majority of your
savvy opponents will charge you the maximum amount
possible to draw to a hand.

Don't Tip Your Hand

Unless you're a super pro, don't ever show a hand that hasn't
been called. If someone asks what you had, say the opposite of the truth, or say something like, "What do you think
I had?" Some people like to say, "I can't recall."

The Importance of Betting with Consistency

Pros always bet confidently, placing the chips in the betting area with speed and a quiet confidence, stating "raise"
whenever we choose that action. The purpose of betting
rapidly is to convey a sense of strength and to engender a
quicker, rather than a well thought out, reaction from an
opponent. But the key is to be boringly consistent when
betting or raising, so as not to provide a tell that your opponents can glom onto and use to decipher your hand. The
way you look at your cards, cover your cards, check or call,
or place your money in the pot is the only part of your
game that should be consistent. You must not be consistent with the way you play your hands.

A good strategy is to pay attention to yourself. Like a
champion bowler who strives for perfect consistency, always cover your cards with a chip and put your hand and
face in the same position. Direct your eyes to the same
spot. Bet and raise with the same movement of the same

hand. Note that people often *look* at the card that has helped them.

If you're afraid that you're exhibiting tells like this, try wearing a poker hat and sunglasses. Look like a player if you're not. If you have mastered the game and can control your tells, try looking like a newbie if you're a shark. Say, "How much can I raise?" But when you hear a real newbie say that, *fold*!

Another Aspect of Confidence

Sheree's friend reported to her that when he calculated his results, he found that he won so much money in one club that it covered all of his losses at another. He realized that this result was not because the players were necessarily worse in one of the clubs. It was because he felt so much more confident in the club where he often won that he simply played better poker there. From the pillow on your chair to the air quality, it's very important to make yourself as comfortable as possible in order to play your best.

Betting on the Don't

After the flop, your confident bet or raise will usually say, "I have the best hand; you should fold." But you can take down even more pots if you realize that your bet can just as easily say, "You have none of this; I am going to claim this pot as mine." You may have none of it either, but in the right position, with no value to be gained by someone calling with their own nothing, your bet will be just as strong as if you flopped a set. You can bet just as strongly that other people don't have a particular card—for example, a deuce that would give them three of a kind—as much as if you have that card.

Don't overdo this, and you'll be swimming in chips. After all, much of the time the flop won't improve your hand, but it won't help your opponent's either. That leaves a large vacuum in the center of the table, and it's often the first and most confident appearance of aggression that wins the pot.

But you can't take advantage of this ploy too often. Sometimes the flop will appear to hit your opponent and do nothing for you. Just let it be. If you are confronting a number of active opponents, the picture becomes entirely different. Then you can safely assume that if the flop does not help you, it probably helped at least one of your adversaries, and one is all it takes to beat you. Against a multitude of opponents, the opposite side of this coin doesn't work too well either. It's much easier to bluff one opponent than it is to bluff three, four, five, or more. For one thing, the more opponents, the more money there is likely to be in the pot. Therefore, chances are greater that at least one of them will call with even a semblance of a hand just because the pot is so large. And with more opponents, it's far more likely that the flop—which provided absolutely no help to you—will be a godsend to someone else.

Creating and Exploiting Your Table Image

There is much to be gained from creating and exploiting your table image. It is often a good strategy, particularly for a new player or a woman, to cultivate a tight image at the poker table. Then later, when you need to, you can bluff effectively. But do so with much caution, paying attention to the position in which you will have to reveal your cards. You do not ever want to have to show bad cards or an outrageous bluff because once your cover is blown, it will be blown forevermore—or at least for the duration of that session, whichever occurs first—and you will have to change your strategy and playing style dramatically to compensate.

Another style that works well is to cultivate an image as a wild and crazy player. This tack is 180 degrees opposite of cultivating a tight image, which—as "Action" Dan Harrington proved in the 2004 World Series of Poker—is a license to bluff. When you cultivate a wild and crazy image, you won't be able to get away with a bluff because your opponents will call. What the wild and crazy player does, however, is to bet his good hands for value. He knows he'll earn additional bets because of his opponents' tendency to call, instead of fold, whenever he commits money to the pot.

Tight or Loose: What's the Best Image for Me?

Which one works best? Is one right or wrong? We don't think one size fits all. Some people just convey a conservative image by dress, grooming, and countenance. It's tough for them to convince anyone they are wild and crazy guys. Others look loony enough to convey that image without ever having played a single hand. If you have limited acting skills, pick a stereotype that's closest to your own personality and go with it. If you're a conservative, button-downed preppy, make yourself appear to be a very tight player and you'll get away with bluffs with regularity. If you look like a mad scientist or a leftover hippie wondering where the '60s went, make your opponents think that that's the real you. Whenever you bet your good hands, you can be assured of being called by lesser holdings.

What you can't do is work both sides of the street at once. It's impossible to convince your opponents that you're simultaneously a very tight and very loose player. So pick an image and stick with it, at least for the remainder of your playing session. Then enhance it, and watch your opponents tilt just a wee bit. They'll buy into an extreme version of whatever your natural playing style and personality happens to be, and they'll pay you off accordingly.

You may find yourself in another city, at a new club, with all new players. Try out a different table image. Or the first cards that you are dealt may determine your new table image. For example, you may get dealt three monster hands in a row right off the bat. You may never have to show these hands, but you do need to realize that some players at the table will think you're a maniac. Others will think you play too many hands. You'll have to have the goods next time you raise. Figure out how you're regarded and play accordingly.

Play off Your Opponents' View of You

Capitalize on other players' wrong assessments of you. If they think you're a maniac then only bet and raise with big hands or the nuts. You'll take some hits because too many people will call, but you'll also get paid off big time at every single river. So be sure to make those river bets, unless you're afraid that someone who has hit the river will reraise you. Conversely, if the players at the table think you're very tight, you can bluff. Just work hard never to get called with a bad hand. If someone does call you on the river, you may say something like, "I missed my draw." Hope that the next player will claim the pot with a pair so that you can quickly muck your hand. Take note: Bluffers do this regularly.

River Bets

Some players make a bet on the river so they don't have to show their rags. This is a bluff, of sorts. If they're called, they'll still have to show their rags and lose an additional bet. If they're not called, they'll have stolen the pot.

Why the Cards You're Dealt Can Be Irrelevant

Well, they're almost irrelevant. Any player would rather be holding good cards than poor ones. But if you're skilled enough at representing big hands under the right circumstances and adept at deciphering the hand your opponent probably holds, you can frequently get away with bluffing. If you make sure your opponent always sees your good hands and never sees your bluffs, he's likely to come away with the impression that you always have a strong hand when you bet. He'll never suspect that all the while you've been robbing him blind.

The Book of Tells "Tell"

There is hardly a poker player alive who has not at least perused the pages of Mike Caro's deservedly famous *The Book of Tells*. How do we know this? We can tell. New players who have not read the book do exhibit the tells referenced in this excellent book. After two hands, that's obvious. These players are easy to beat, but their presence at the table is usually quite ephemeral. But new players who have read the book make concerted, but usually poor, efforts to do the opposite of what they've read. If they're weak, they'll look away. If they're strong, they'll stare you down. It's beneficial to note that most players, whatever their strategy, are consistent! And notwithstanding all of the famous actors who play the game—McCauley Culkin, James Woods, Gabe Kaplan, and 2005 World Series of Poker women's champion Jennifer Tilly—very few players are good poker actors. Figure out if a particular player has read the *Book of Tells* and is trying to bamboozle you with reverse psychology and you'll know whether to call, fold, or raise.

Develop a working theory about each player. If you're out of the hand, bet with yourself about who is going to win that pot. Who is truly confident and who is feigning confidence? Test your theory one player at a time.

And as for yourself, be inconsistent!

Acting Technique

Let's say you're at the river and you're interested in trying to take down the pot with a bluff. You're sure that if you can convince your opponent that the river card made your straight, he'll fold. Instead of overacting or using *Book of Tells* reverse psychology, try thinking to yourself, "Excellent, that last card made my straight. Way to go!" Just think it hard enough to believe it yourself while you're making your bet. Don't overact. Just try to make it a real thought. If you have to look at something, look wherever you would normally look if you weren't conscious of tells and if that card really did make your hand. Perhaps you'll look at your opponent's chips. Perhaps you'll look at the river card. Perhaps you'll look at the TV. If you don't know what you'd look at, then try to pay attention to yourself the next time the river card does complete your straight.

Similarly, if you're making a value bet on the river and you want your opponent to call with an inferior hand—you know her hand is inferior because you have the nuts—try thinking, "Please don't call. Please don't call. It would be really terrible for me if you'd call. Please, for heavensakes, fold!" If your opponent is one who likes to study you before making a decision, you'll find this technique will work like a charm. Just don't do it every time. Next time you want that same player to call, try thinking, "Please call." What a pleasure it will be when they do.

Why Women Often Have an Edge

Women can have an edge because they are usually underrated by men, often played down to, and flirted with much of the time. Many men just don't believe that women can play tough, aggressive poker. They also don't believe most women will ever bluff. Many of the best women players take advantage of these opportunities by flirting back with their male admirers. Then they skewer them when they have the best of it. Women who are able to read men's intentions—and most of the time these intentions are embarrassingly obvious—can easily manipulate their male opponents into making foolish plays and then take full advantage of the situation.

When men see women as straightforward players who seldom ever bluff, who respond to their flirtatious charms, they are playing right into their hands. Some men won't raise a woman out of some misguided sense of gallantry—or perhaps it's merely a continuation of the flirting instinct—and in so doing deviate from the kind of play that wins the money. Call it what you will, but the rules of attraction are sometimes much stronger than the inclinations of poker. Whenever that happens—sometimes orchestrated by a female player, sometimes not—it's generally the guy who winds up slinking away to lick his wounds.

Self-Invented Tells

Sheree remembers her first Las Vegas tournament at the Mirage. She was at the final table with a man who was deciding whether to call her bet. He paused and stared at her. Sheree looked him directly in the eye and gave him a sparkle. He decided to call, and Sheree won the pot with a big hand. A little later, Sheree saw that she needed chips. She decided to bluff that player at a pivotal moment in the tournament. Again, she made a raise. Again, he gave her a stare. And again, she sparkled. The man decided to fold—never realizing that Sheree was bluffing. That hand crippled the man's chip stack and caused him to be the next person to be eliminated from the final table. Sheree went on to take second place and received her first 1099 for poker wins. Take note of people who examine you and remember to use your own self-invented tells.

If You Look Weak on the River, Someone Will "Bet and Take It"

If everyone checks on the flop, it might be a sign that no one has a particularly strong hand. It might also mean that one opponent is checking a big hand on an inexpensive betting round in order to induce a bet on the turn. The cost of betting usually doubles here and opponents can be trapped by check-raising. But if all your opponents check the turn and the river card is not a third card of the same suit—and if it's not, no flush is possible—and does not otherwise look threatening, chances are good that no one has a very strong hand.

Professional poker players call this an abandoned pot. When you find yourself in this situation, you might just want to come out betting. Unless that river card gave an opponent two pair or better, or you're confronting at least one opponent who is always going to call to "keep you honest," a bet on your behalf stands a good chance of capturing the pot. It's also always interesting to watch your opponents fold in turn like a row of dominos tumbling down.

Even though some of your more astute opponents will realize you're probably stealing the pot, they usually won't call you if they don't have the goods. After all, the operative

word here is "probably," and since they're never completely certain about the hand you're holding, the vast majority of players will fold to a bet. Every now and then
you'll find a tough, aggressive player who will raise your
bluff with a bluff of his own. But that happens so infrequently that it's not even worth worrying about. If you find
yourself up against an opponent capable of making this
kind of play, we'd recommend staying out of his way unless
you really have a big hand, at which point we'll assume
you'll reraise the next time he tries this play against you.

Make a Play for Abandoned Pots; If You Don't, Someone Else Will

We've talked about abandoned pots throughout this book
because it's an important concept. While much of the time
poker resembles a conflict between two gladiators, it's also
true that quite often there is no conflict at all. Each opponent's actions seem to say, "Take the pot . . . please." Whenever you can identify a pot just sitting there about to be
abandoned, you need to step up and snatch it away from
anyone else who may be a day late and a dollar short with
the same intentions. Just the ability to do this once or
twice a session can turn a break-even player into a winner.
An abandoned pot is like finding a mobster bag man's
satchel full of unmarked bills in the backseat of a cab. When
you see it, take it and get out of town as quickly as possible.
Remember, one of poker's operative mottos: If the shoe fits,
steal it!

"I'll Take the Tournament Win for a Million, Alex"

The world seems to be divided between those who love
games and those who don't love games. Those who do love

games, like Sheree, can't get enough of them. She'll frequently turn non-game situations into games and look for every opportunity to create games within games. When she's watching the TV show *Jeopardy* ™, for example, or *Wheel of Fortune* ™, which she was a contestant on, she begins each show by guessing who is going to win. Sheree has a great record of predicting the winner. It's almost always the one who is alert and relaxed at the beginning of the show, the one who is the most comfortable talking about him or herself during the interview with Alex Trebeck and Pat Sajak. Sheree does this at the poker table as well, and we recommend that you do the same. When you're playing poker, guess who is going to win. Guess who is going to "give back" their chips or steadily lose them. The better you get at this guessing game, the better you'll be at poker and the more chips you'll take home at the end of the night.

Obvious Tilt

People tell you when they're on tilt—just in case you didn't happen to notice. Take note of someone who raises right after they took a beat, or one who says, "This is a tilt raise." Players handle their bad beats very differently. Some players, when they lose a hand that they feel they should have won, tuck their tails between their legs and whimper away like a puppy dog. Others take the opposite tack and tend to come out raising in a flagrant attempt to get themselves even immediately—each and every time they lose a pot. Some players will only say they're on tilt because they're not. Some players will tell you they're on tilt as an excuse to play 2–4 offsuit to the river. Once you get a fix on which way your opponents tend to go, you can use it to your advantage time and time again.

Leave Your Ego at the Door

If you're a good player, learn how to make them think you're not. They'll come after your chips and you will take their chips. They will be left scratching their heads about how they lost to a bad player. This is because no way will their ego allow them to change their wrong assessment about you. Just prepare to be hated!

Not Everyone Is Going to Like You Anyway

In 1995, when the late Ken Flaton was vying for the championship title in Atlantic City, he was confronted with a choice that made him most unpopular. One of the players at the final table, a veteran player, suddenly needed to relieve himself in the bathroom. He kindly asked the other players for permission to step out since the tournament rules did not allow for the clock to be stopped before the end of the hour. All of the players except Ken said, "Sure, we'll hold up play till you get back," but Ken refused. He said, "No," and explained later that this man knew from experience how to pace himself. He should have known not to drink so much coffee. If he had to go while the game played on, he was free to do that, but the tournament did not have to stop for him. The blinds were high and the championship was at stake. What happened was that the other players at the table, as a favor, played so slowly that the man did have time to go and return. The man came back angry at Ken and on tilt. Ken ended up winning the tournament. Ken looked at this as an example of using the rules to your advantage. If enforcing a rule puts another player on tilt, so much the better. Not everyone would agree that Ken did the right thing. Outside of poker, most people would consider Ken's actions cruel. But within the boundaries of the game, many would say that what he did was not only acceptable but essential. What do you think?

People Are Predictable

At least they are most of the time. Poker players are no different than anyone else on this planet. We all fall into habitual patterns of behavior, default positions, as it were. They enable us to deal with many of life's prosaic choices on autopilot, and without giving them too much thought.

We're that way at the card table, too. Many players will call rather than fold or raise. It's a predictable pattern of behavior. And when you can spot this kind of behavior in one of your opponents, then any time she acts contrary to this, you have a view of some anomalous behavior that jumps out at you like a bright spotlight on a dark night. Something's happened to make this player respond in a manner that's different from her usual betting pattern. If she raises when she usually calls, you can throw all but your very best hands away. If she's a habitual raiser who just calls, you have to wonder if she is playing a really weak hand, or has a very strong one, and is acting out of character with her real self in order to lure you into a bet. Wait until she comes back over the top and check-raises, garnering an additional bet for her guile.

The Power of Knowledge and Practice

Knowledge is knowledge; experience is experience. One can read every book on the shelf and sit down and play a decent game, but no one can play stellar poker without reading every book and doing considerable time at the table, testing one's mettle in a variety of situations—day in and day out—and then rereading the books. One day, everything you've read will suddenly come together like a cake that has risen perfectly in the oven. Turning book knowledge and experience into cash is like no frosting you've ever tasted. The experienced players who have also read all the books are the best of the best.

You Can't Overdo It

If you've just raised several hands in a row and you look down under the gun and see a big hand, you might just want to limp. If you raise yet again, you're going to get too many callers. You may have to see the flop, and see if you hit the flop, before you decide how to proceed from there.

Be a Master of Many Disguises

Because balance, disguise, and deception are necessary staples of winning poker—well, they're really not required if your opponents are brain dead or completely unobservant about your hands and how you play them—top echelon play means disguising your play. Not all the time, mind you; you don't even have to do it most of the time. But you've got to have a change-up in your arsenal and you have to use it *some* of the time. Otherwise, the hitters will all sit there waiting for your fast ball and the good ones will know what to do with it when it comes.

Disguising your play can take one of two basic forms: You can play good hands as though they were somewhat weaker than they really are, or you can play some of your other hands just like they're pocket kings or aces.

In fixed limit games, you have fewer weapons at your disposal. You're limited to checking or betting if no one has acted yet, or folding, calling, or raising if someone else has already bet. In pot-limit and no-limit games, you have the additional consideration of how much to bet and how much to raise. Both give you an opportunity to either create or negate the right price for your opponent to continue with a draw, if he has one. It will also make him consider the quality of his hand, compared to the hand you're representing, by virtue of the size of your bet or raise.

After the flop, math may dictate how much to bet. But what should you do before the flop, when it's not quite so clear what anyone else has?

- If your opponent is a tight, timid player, the kind who can be driven off all but his very best hands by a nice-sized bet, you are better off playing your best hands for their own intrinsic value. Add to that mix by playing some of your less-than-best-hands that way too. Because your opponent's propensity is to toss hands away, you'll be building some bluffing opportunities into the disguise you're using to cloak your really good hands. If your standard raise in a no-limit game is three or four times the big blind, then that's the way you should bet your pocket kings, pocket aces, pocket queens, and a few other hands, too.

- If your opponent is a very aggressive player, you should still bet most of your good hands for value. You should also underplay them every so often. Underplaying encourages your aggressive opponent to do your betting for you. If you've begun with a big pocket pair and the flop is not devastating to your hand, you can let your opponent do your betting for you and snap him off for a couple of additional bets when the time is right. There is a drawback to doing this too often. If you always look to trap and check-raise your opponent, he may become wary of betting into you all the time. Your frequent check-raises will serve to make a better player out of him, at least when he's up against you. As a consequence, he'll present fewer opportunities for you to snap off his bets.

- When your opponent is someone who approaches poker with an "If you bet, I raise; if you raise, I reraise" attitude, you're never going to make a better player out of him. He is operating at the polar extreme of maniacal aggressiveness and doesn't ever want to come in from the cold, nevermind the fact that he probably doesn't care one whit about your hand. Not him. He just wants to raise. Your job is to let him stay there. Bet your good hands, and hope he raises so you can get him committed for three bets before he even sees the flop. While most experts all agree that you want aggressive players seated to your right, so you can isolate on their raises by reraising with your very best hands, this is a guy you want on your left. If all goes according to plan, you'll bet, he'll raise, and all the other players will discount his raises. After all, when someone raises every hand, wouldn't you begin to doubt the quality of the cards he's holding? The other opponents will cold call two bets from him, just like they were calling one bet from a more temperate player. Then you can three-bet him and you'll have all those other callers right where you want them, trapped in the sunshine for three bets with nowhere to go.

- If your opponent is a good, solid, selective player, just like you, you're far better off adding some hands to broaden out your best hands, and then bet them for value. If your opponent is straightforward, solid, good, and spends time trying to discern what you are holding, as well as trying to determine what you think he has, get the best value you can out of your very good hands. But you'll have to bluff some of the time, else your skillful opponents will begin to duck when you roll out the heavy artillery and keep their heads down until you cease firing. By bluffing, they'll have to consider that you might not always have the hand you're representing. If you are able to bluff correctly, you will get some calls that you would never have gotten if you were one of those real rocks who hasn't bluffed since the Cubbies won the pennant. When you bluff at the correct frequency, there's just not much your opponent can do about it.

4

HANDS

Poker ultimately comes down to hands. It's always about hands, when all is said and done. Turn over the better hand and you're the winner. Win more money on your good hands, while possessing sufficient discipline to lose less with your weaker hands, and you'll walk away a big winner in the long run.

Deciding if you're going to see the flop with your first two cards is probably the most important decision you'll make playing hold'em. Learning what to do with your first two cards is not all that difficult. After all, there are only 169 two-card starting combinations and you certainly shouldn't play all of them.

Hand Characteristics

Each combination has certain unique characteristics that render your two starting cards either more or less playable. There are five basic hand categories: pairs, connected cards, gapped cards, suited connectors, or suited gapped cards.

Unless they're paired, your cards will either be suited or unsuited. Both suited and unsuited cards can be connected (adjacent to one another) or gapped. Examples of connectors are J-T, 5-4, and 4-3. Unconnected cards might be one-, two-, three-gapped, or more, and would include holdings such as: Q-T, 8-5, 6-2, or 7-2. The size of the gap is important and the reason has to do with straights. Although you can make a straight with one-, two-, or three-gapped cards, the smaller the gap, the easier it is to make a straight—with a few significant exceptions.

If you are dealt a three-gapped hand such as 10-6, the only three cards that will allow you to build a straight are 9-8-7. But if you were dealt 10-9, a straight can be made with K-Q-J, Q-J-8, J-8-7, and 8-7-6. The only exceptions to this rule occur at both ends of the card-rank spectrum. A-K, for example, make one straight and one only. Because there are no cards higher in rank than an ace, Q-J-T are the only three ranks of cards that will complete a straight with A-K. A-2 is in the same boat. Only 5-4-3 makes a bottom straight. Although both A-K and A-2 are *connectors*, and not gapped, each of them can only make one straight.

In similar fashion, K-Q and 3-2 are also constrained and each of these hands can only make a straight with A-J-T and J-T-9, or A-4-5 or 6-5-4 respectively. Q-J and 4-3 are also limited, and each of these combinations can make three straights. Q-J needs A-K-T, K-T-9, or T-9-8, while 4-3 is similar. All other connectors can make straights four ways, which is a big advantage over gapped cards.

Guidelines for Playing Your Hands

Here are three simple guidelines to guide your decision about whether to play your first two cards.

- Cards that are neither suited nor paired, unconnected, and four-gapped or larger should never be played under normal circumstances.

- Play few hands in early position.
- Suited cards are more valuable than unsuited cards of equal rank.

Because acting later in a hand is more advantageous than acting early, you can afford to see the flop with weaker hands in late position. In fact, if you're last to act, you'll have the advantage of seeing how each of your opponents act on the current round of betting. That's important because some starting hands play better against a large number of opponents, while others play better heads-up. Late position also tells you who's representing and the later you act, the more information you'll have at your disposal.

Position Is Even More Important in Big-Bet Poker

In no-limit or pot-limit games, acting last is even more important. This is because of *implied odds*, which can be thought of as the ratio of *what you think you will win*—and this includes money that will probably be wagered on subsequent rounds—to the cost of a current bet. Here's how this works. Suppose there's $20 in the pot and your opponent bets $20. The current odds offered by the pot are $40 ($20 in the pot plus the $20 your opponent just wagered) to $20 (your cost to call). $40-to-$20 is the equivalent of 2-to-1.

But if you estimate that your opponent will pay off a $100 bet if you make your hand, your implied odds are not 2-to-1. They are $140-to-$20, or 7-to-1. The latter is a lot more attractive than the 2-to-1 *current odds*, which is why no-limit and pot-limit games are often predicated on implied odds. But in fixed limit games, where your next wager can never be as large a multiple of the current wager as it so often is in a no-limit or pot-limit game, the concept of implied odds, although still important, is not as significant.

With the right implied odds, you can afford to see the flop in pot- and no-limit games for one bet with some relatively weak hands. If you're lucky, and the flop hits one of these marginal hands twice or three times, you can bet big with the potential of trapping opponents for most or all of their chips because the strength of your hand will be significantly disguised.

If you saw the flop with a weak hand, such as 5♠4♠ against three others, and the flop was 3-2-A or K-5-4, you figure to have the best hand on the flop. Anyone with an ace in his hand will call your bet or come out betting into your straight if he acts before you. And when you flop two pair, you should get action from anyone holding a king in his hand.

These hands are not completely immune to danger. In the last case, a running pair on the last two cards would give the player with a king in his hand two bigger pair than yours. You do figure to be in the lead on the flop, however, and the odds favor you winning the pot by hand's end.

Hands You Can Play Anytime

Aces: When you're dealt a pair of aces, no one has a stronger hand than you. If someone bets, go ahead and raise. If there's a bet and a raise in front of you, feel free to reraise. There's not a hand out there right now that's better than yours.

Kings: Kings are a favorite against any hand except a pair of aces, and as long as an ace doesn't flop, you are probably still in the lead.

With kings, as well as with queens and jacks, flop awareness is critical. Many hold'em players, especially in fixed limit games, will call with any ace, no matter how weak the side card is that accompanies it. If you do this, you should be concerned any time an ace hits the board. That doesn't mean you should fold if an ace appears, and you'd almost never fold if you were heads-up. But with two or more opponents, your kings might be doomed if there is a bet and a call, and especially if there's a raise before it's your turn to act.

Queens and Jacks: A pair of queens or jacks is *probably* the best hand before the flop. But if bigger cards appear on the flop, you're in jeopardy.

Because queens or jacks are much more vulnerable than aces and kings, defense is important. If you can narrow the field, you're better off. Raise or reraise when it's your turn to act. If you can eliminate any opponent holding an ace, or a king with a weak kicker, you significantly increase your chance of winning.

Middle Pairs—Tens, Nines, Eights, Sevens: Even with a pair of tens, which is the best of these holdings, sixteen cards can give one of your opponents a higher pair. It's more likely than not that at least one overcard will appear on the flop. The fewer adversaries you go up against with these hands, the better off you are.

Other Hands Playable in Early Position

Many players treat big-suited connected cards, such as A-K, A-Q and K-Q like they were aces or kings. But there's a big difference. A pocket pair has *immediate* value. With connectors, you *hope* to make a hand, and all you have now is potential, which isn't always realized.

Even when you begin with a hand as strong as A-K, you'll flop an ace or a king only about one-third of the time. If you keep this in mind, you shouldn't have any trouble folding hands like these when warranted. That's a big edge over those opponents who rarely fold these hands, regardless of the flop and the subsequent betting action.

Flush potential is the difference between big suited and unsuited connectors. While you won't make a flush that often, flopping a flush draw, which happens approximately 10 percent of the time, keeps you in the hunt and allows you to continue contesting the pot. You may not make your flush but you might back into top pair with top kicker and win the pot that way. If you flop a four-flush and catch an ace or a king instead of your flush card on the turn, you'll have top pair plus the added equity of a live flush draw. Part of the value of suited connectors is that they often allow you to remain in the pot and win, by means other than completing your primary draw.

Playable Hands in Middle and Late Position

You can add a pair of sixes and a pair of fives to your playable repertoire in middle position. But with small and middling pairs, your objective is always the same: Get in cheaply and either flop a set or get out.

Whenever your opponents routinely play any suited ace, you can play A-9 suited through A-6 suited, and your hand will usually be the best ace if no one raised before the flop, since most players in games like these will raise with an A-T suited or better.

But A-8 suited, A-7 suited, and A-6 suited are still dangerous hands, even in middle position, and you want to avoid flopping an ace and finding yourself outkicked.

Unsuited cards like K-T, Q-J, Q-T, J-T can also be played for one bet only. You should never, however, cold-call a raise with hands like these. King-ten is especially dangerous in a raised pot when a king flops. Because so many players raise with hands like A-K, K-Q and often K-J, if you call with K-T, you'll have no idea whether yours is the best hand.

Hands You Can Play in Late Position

Late position offers you the advantage of seeing how most of your opponents played their hands. If someone raised, you can fold any hand you'd play only in unraised pots. You also have the advantage of knowing with certainty whether you are taking the flop with a large or small number of opponents. Some hands, like smaller suited connectors, can only be profitably played in unraised pots with a large number of opponents. Others, like pairs, play better when you can narrow your opponents to a few.

If this concept is true for fixed-limit games, it is even truer for pot- and no-limit games. The number of opponents bears significantly on the implied odds you will receive if you play a marginal hand but are fortunate enough to catch a miraculous flop

Acting last is advantageous because of the knowledge at your disposal. When you act late, or in last position, you never have to wonder if you'll be raised, or guess at the number of opponents who will be taking the flop with you. In late position you have this information at your disposal, and that's a big edge.

You can also play any pair, providing the pot has not been raised before it's your turn to act. Go ahead and play deuces, treys, and fours as long as you can do so for one bet. While there's no chance you'll have top pair on the flop, you're hoping to flop a set or an open-ended straight draw. You might even raise with a small pair if you have just one caller. Raising might cause the blinds to fold, and even if the flop misses you but an ace or a king flops, you can come out betting, just the same as if you raised with A-K and the flop fit your hand like a glove.

You can do the same thing with any suited ace. While you'd love to flop a flush with this hand, you'll have to play carefully if an ace appears. Other connectors, suited or not, can be played on the cheap whenever you've got lots of opponents who will presumably pay you off when you make a big hand

Selectivity is the key to successful play. Keep yourself in situations offering favorable pot odds. When you're in a favorable situation, be aggressive. Bet to get more money in the pot when you have a big hand or to eliminate competition when you're holding the kind of hand that plays best against fewer opponents.

Ace-Nine and Similar Trash

In games with better players, such as mid-limit games of $10–$20 and up, A-9 and below is a money loser. As a result most pros also eschew *ace-little*. Just because you occasionally win with a horrible hand, and just because you see other people win with horrible cards, you will make far more over the long term by almost never playing hands that you know are horrible. If this seems at odds with the advice on the past few pages, it's all a function of game texture. Some hands are money winners in one style game, but are money losers in others. With practice you'll develop a feel for those hands that can be added, or must be subtracted, for your playing repertoire. Bringing in hands and eliminating others depending on game texture is one of the hallmarks of a good professional player. While you might not have this skill fully developed right now, you should always be examining game texture with an eye to adding some and eliminating other hands.

One reason not to play little cards, that is, cards below a ten, is that even when you flop two pairs or a straight, they often don't hold up to the river. Some of the more common confrontations you see all the time in hold'em games are shown below. One reason to avoid playing small cards most of the time is to avoid finding yourself on the long shot end of these confrontations.

One Pair and Overcards

When the announcer says, "It's a race," he's talking about the kind of showdown commonly found in no-limit tournaments when one player has a pair and his opponent has two bigger cards. Ace-king versus a pair of jacks is an example of just this sort of race. The pair is about a 55 percent to 45 percent favorite, so it's not really a neck-and-neck race. In fact, in a presidential election this kind of victory would be considered a landslide. But in poker, it's a race. Although the pair is favored, the two big cards are only a 1.2-to-1 dog, and they win enough of the time so that it's a dicey situation for both participants. And what makes it dicey is that when you're all-in, your tournament life is predicated on something that at 1.2-to-1 is a little closer than you'd like. When you have to risk your tournament life, you'd prefer to be at least a 2-to-1 favorite.

High Pair and Low Pair

A bigger pair is more than an 80 percent favorite to win, or about a 4-to-1 favorite over a lower pair. These numbers can vary a bit, depending on the relationship between the pairs and their suits. If you have K♠K♦ and your opponent has Q♠Q♦, you are a bigger favorite than you would be if your opponent's pair of queens were both of different suits than your kings. When your cards are the same suit as your opponent's, he can never win by making a flush. If there's a flush, you'll win because you'll have the bigger one. Having your pair the same suit as your opponent's smaller pair adds about 1.5 percent to your edge. It's not much, but every little bit helps.

One Pair and Two Lower Cards

This is a much more comfortable situation for the pair than when he's up against two bigger cards. Against two smaller cards, the pair is approximately a 5-to-1 favorite, and the two lower cards, which will need to make at least two pair to win, are a decided long shot.

One Pair and One Up–One Down

What happens when your opponent has one card that's bigger and one that's smaller than your pair? You're really trying to duck the chance that your opponent pairs his overcard, which is really what's needed for him to win. He can also win by catching two of his smaller cards or making a straight, but those chances are scant. Your pair eliminates two of the cards he'll need to complete his straight, and making trips with one smaller card is a long shot, too. Just pairing his smaller card does your opponent no good. To win, he'll usually need to pair his overcard, and if he does, you still have a chance—although it's a long shot—to redraw on him.

Two Higher Cards and Two Lower Cards

Two higher cards are favored over two lower ones, but not by as much as you might think. They're about a 5-to-3 favorite—almost 2-to-1, but not quite. When you're looking at A-K versus 6-5, you'd think that a hand as pretty as Big Slick should be a prohibitive favorite. But it usually boils down to the fact that the hand making a pair becomes the winner.

If your pair is adjacent to your opponent's lower pair, such as kings versus queens as opposed to kings versus eights, your edge increases, albeit slightly. Adjacency reduces the number of straights a lower pair might make.

Small Pairs and Smallish Connectors

Playing small pocket pairs properly can be difficult, and what to do when you're dealt smallish connectors is not a walk in the park either.

Small pairs, and we're talking about a pair of sevens or lower, can be thought of as drawing hands much of the time, though there are exceptions to this guideline. And if you think of them that way, you shouldn't go too far wrong. After all, a big pair, like aces, kings, or queens, frequently wins without improving. They're that good. But a small pair usually needs help. And other than sticking its nose in the midst of a 7-6-4 flop and getting lucky on the turn or river, a pair of fives can only improve by flopping a set.

The nice thing about flopping a set is that it will cost your opponent some chips by the time he comes to grips with the possibility that you're holding three-of-a-kind. There's not much he's going to be able to do about it either. The other side of this coin is that the odds against flopping a set when you're dealt a pocket pair are 7.5-to-1, which means it's not going to happen all that often, and that's another reason why big pocket pairs are so much more desirable than their smallish cousins.

Keep the Cost Low When Drawing to a Small Pair

When you have a hand that's a long shot, and drawing to improve a small pair against two or more opponents certainly falls into that category, keep the cost as low as possible. From a strategic perspective you're a lot better off playing a small pair for one bet than cold-calling two bets in a raised pot. The message is clear: A raise is a statement that your opponent holds a big hand. While it might be nothing more than two big cards, it may contain a pair bigger than your pair of fives, which makes it a prohibitive favorite.

But when you act in late position, you have an opportunity to see whether any of your opponents have raised before it's your turn to decide what to do with your cards. If someone raises, you can safely toss your small pair away. Otherwise, if there are a few callers, you can see the flop for one bet. If you get lucky and hit your set, you're in good shape.

If the flop misses you and the eyes of face cards are staring up at you—just toss your hand away if anyone bets. Against a relatively large field, chances are pretty good that flop will help someone, and if that someone isn't you, your unimproved pair of fives is now an also-ran.

When Is a Small Pair a Drawing Hand and When Is It Not?

But if no one has called the blinds when it's your turn to act, you can raise from late position because your pair of fives figures to be the favorite against whatever random cards the two blinds might hold.

Do you see what's happening here? Against a scattering of opponents, who hold good enough hands to voluntarily

commit money to the pot, your pair of fives is really drawing to improve. Against one or two opponents, who hold
random cards in their hands and have to post a blind bet
like-it-or-not, you probably have the best hand. You ought
to raise with it, in hopes of winning the confrontation right
there or stealing the pot by betting regardless of whether the
flop was any help to you or not.

And what about connectors? Well, they're drawing
hands under any circumstances, and in a heads-up situation even A-K is a slight underdog to any pocket pair. But as
a general rule everyone raises with big connectors like A-K
and that turns out to be a pretty good idea. An ace or a king
will flop when you're holding Big Slick roughly one-third
of the time. When it does, it guarantees that Big Slick has
flopped top pair with the very best kicker, and that's a
moneymaking hand in most hold'em games. Even if you
miss the flop completely and your raise was only called by
the big blind—after all, he's already in for one bet, so he's
getting a "discount" to call you—you might have the best
hand even if you don't improve.

Why Smallish Connectors Are So Vulnerable

But we're talking smallish connectors here, not Big Slick. If
you hold 9-8 suited, you'll flop a nine or an eight about
one third of the time. But unlike Big Slick, hitting the flop
with 9-8 doesn't guarantee much of anything. For starters,
you may not flop the highest pair, particularly if bigger
cards appear. Even when you flop the top pair, your hand is
vulnerable to the same pair with a bigger kicker. Actually,
vulnerable isn't a strong enough word. Your hand is *dominated* by the same pair with a bigger kicker. Unless you can
make a straight or flush on the turn or the river, you are

drawing in hopes of pairing your kicker, and there are only three cards of that rank unaccounted for in the deck.

With smallish connectors, you're hoping the flop hits you twice—three times would be even better—before you feel comfortable with your hand. That means you're looking for a four-flush, four to a straight, trips, or two pair, and these are all long shots.

Requirements for Playing Small Pairs and Smallish Connectors

What are the strategic implications of looking for a long shot in this situation? You will usually play smallish connectors much as you'd play a small pair. You want a relatively large number of opponents who will pay you off when you get lucky, and because your hand is a long shot, you need to play it for one bet only. The only way to guarantee such conditions is to play hands like these from late position. If you play them early, you run the risk of someone raising behind you. And even if there is no raise, you may not get the number of customers you need to justify your investment.

Unlike a small pocket pair, smallish suited connectors probably won't be favored over two random blind hands, and if you are the first player to enter the pot with hands like these, you are bluffing; you're not betting for value as you would be with a small pocket pair against the blinds.

With hands like these, you're drawing to improve and if you don't get any help on the flop, you stand a good chance of having to release your hand. So as long as you're playing a hand that needs to improve, try making it as inexpensive for yourself as possible. When you do play small pairs and smallish connectors, play 'em late, and on the cheap.

It's worth noting that these kinds of hands can sometimes be more valuable in no-limit and pot-limit games. While the mathematical parameters surrounding drawing hands won't change from game to game, the pot odds just might. When betting can escalate exponentially, as it can in these games, the implied odds that accrue when you hit your hand and no one realizes it means that you don't have to win many of these confrontations to make them profitable in the long run.

5

MONEY

A poker philosopher once said that, "Poker is a game of people played with money." And he's probably right. At any rate, poker is much more than just a game of cards. Money is not only how you keep score in poker, it's the language of the game, too. Money—or more precisely, chips and their movement into and out of the pot—is how poker players communicate during a game. We don't tell another player, "I've got a big hand; get out of the pot." We raise, or reraise. And the message is sent and delivered with nary a word spoken.

For a professional poker player money is also his capital, just as a factory and trucks are capital for a manufacturer. There's a big difference between capital and income, and we'll explain it all to you while debunking some of the foolish money management theories you hear all the time in casinos.

Money makes the world go round in a poker room just as much as it does in other aspects of life—maybe even more so.

Bubble, Double, Toil and Trouble

Ya gotta want it! When you sit down at any poker table, you have to be the one who wants to win the most. Try thinking of your chips as rare and precious magical coins, with magnetic properties to attract more chips. Never let go of your resolve to make each session a winning session. It won't always happen, but if you're determined and have the tools of a good poker player, it will happen more often than not and make you a long-term winner. Keep good records and be honest with yourself. Are you winning overall or losing? Did you win $200 last night or $183? Now don't lie! If it's yourself you are deceiving, who is the winner?

You're Not a Good Player Unless You're Winning

One can play well and lose in the short run, but over time . . . good players beat bad players. That's just the way it is. Poker is a funny game. If a rank amateur were to sit down with one of the legends of the game and play one hand of poker, anything could happen and the amateur stands an even chance of coming out ahead in that confrontation. But if they were to play for a long time—a day, a week, a month, a year, or even a lifetime—chance favors the legend, and the reason is simple. He'll win far more money with his good hands and lose much less with his poor ones than our amateur. And the longer they played, the more you can be certain that the amateur would be ground down by the skilled professional.

This doesn't happen in other endeavors. Even a single hole of golf against a top touring pro would show most of us up as complete duffers, and we'd have no chance at all. Wanna take a cut at a major league fastball? Don't waste your time. Whether we took one swing or spent the next month flailing away in the batter's box, our chances of success would be slim. And it only gets worse from there. If you like really slim chances, spend one round in the ring with a professional boxer, or play a game of chess with a grandmaster. You'll have no chance in either endeavor, though in chess, only your pride figures to take a beating.

But things are different in poker, and it's these illusions and occasional victories that keep poor poker players returning to play again and again. Even the very worst players manage to win on occasion, and sometimes the better player is just not on his or her game and plays down to, or even below, the level of his opponents. But over the long haul, if you're not winning, you're not a good player. You might be a good player against a different set of opponents, but unless you can regularly beat the game you're playing in, you'll either need to improve your chops or find a softer game, usually at lower betting limits.

Calling Stations Are Your Chip Source

When you first sit down, fold almost everything. Watch who plays the most hands. Chances are this will be your chip source. The player who plays the most hands will win the most pots, but will also lose the most pots and the most money, too. Unless someone is dealt a remarkable run of good hands, an opponent who plays too many hands is entering many pots with very weak holdings, and you can take his money by betting your good hands for value with the anticipation that he will call and you will win.

This Is a Stick-up

It's important to remember that money is a poker player's weapon of choice. Professional poker players regard money as *capital*, while professionals in most other fields regard it as *income*, and that's a point worth remembering. When you dip into your poker bankroll to get some spending cash, you are converting capital into income. That's like a business deciding to sell off some of their delivery trucks in order to raise cash. While it provides cash, it's a one-time thing, and once depleted it's gone and you won't have that money any longer.

Consider that strapped-for-cash company that's contemplating selling off some of its delivery trucks. Although that firm will have some cash on hand, they've no way to replenish the capital they'll so desperately need to keep their business afloat. And poker's no different. If you deplete your bankroll, you'll be playing in smaller games or playing on "scared money" in bigger ones. That's usually a prescription for disaster.

Be the Bettor, Not the Caller

The default action of choice for most players is to call. Can't decide what to do? Don't know whether your hand is the best or not? Have four cards to a straight or a flush? Most players will call, often without even thinking about it. What the experts know, and most other players don't, is that betting or raising is usually a far superior strategy to checking and calling. Here's why. If I call, I can win only by showing down the best hand. But by betting or raising, I have two ways to win. I might have the best hand or the aggressive action I've taken might cause my opponent to fold his hand. He might fold a better hand than mine or he might fold a hand that could improve when the next card is dealt. All the best players share one common trait. They are aggressive. They temper that aggression by being selective—unmitigated aggression is, after all, the asphalt that paves the road to ruin—but selective aggression is a quality that separates top players from run-of-the-mill, recreational players.

And how do most players know what to do? They have a set of starting hand standards for each game. Players who have learned David Sklansky's starting hand groupings, or Lou Krieger's recommended starting hand standards, have a powerful edge on those who have to deal with each decision about playing or folding as though it were something new that they've never encountered before.

Although skilled players know when and how to deviate from the "book" move, they do have these guidelines to carry them through the murky waters of deciding which hands to risk money on.

Don't Play with the Rent Money

This is so true that we shouldn't even have to mention it, but we will. Don't risk money you can't afford to lose. Even if you're playing with a table full of fish that you can beat eight days a week and twice on Sunday, bear in mind that there are no guarantees of winning when it comes to poker. You should never play for stakes you can't afford, even if you are a prohibitive favorite in the game. Here's the general rule of poker, and all forms of gambling for that matter. The stakes should be big enough to hurt, but not crush you, if you lose.

If the stakes are so small that they have no meaning, then there's no governor to keep you playing your best poker. If we were playing penny poker, where the most you could expect to lose in a session would be five dollars, it would be tough to maintain the discipline to play good, solid poker, because a five-dollar loss or win would have no meaning to most of us. If we were playing in a game where the stakes were so high that a loss would equate to a few months' salary, the stakes would be too high and we couldn't play our normal, aggressive game for fear of losing too much money.

Find Betting Limits That Are Right for You

Somewhere you'll find betting limits that are perfect for you, and you need to figure that out so that you're comfortable with your game. Bill Gates has been seen at the Bellagio in Las Vegas playing poker in a game with betting limits of three and six dollars. People walking by were astounded that the world's richest man was essentially playing for matchsticks. But if stakes have to have some meaning, Bill Gates is in a league populated by very few others. What are appropriate stakes for someone of his wealth? Should he play poker for betting limits of $250,000–$500,000? Or maybe a little more? Even though he might be able to afford these stakes, it's not easy to find a game like this. It probably doesn't exist. Gates, secure in the knowledge that for all practical purposes none of the stakes he could find on a typical day in Las Vegas would really be meaningful to a man of his wealth, is as comfortable playing $3–$6 as he would be playing $2,000–$4,000.

If you're in Bill Gates's financial league, it won't matter what stakes you select either. But if you're like most of us, somewhere there are betting limits that work for your own financial and psychological circumstances. Here's the litmus test that works for most poker players: A loss should hurt, but should not cripple us; while a win should be exhilarating. And don't bet the rent money whatever you do.

How Much Is Luck; How Much Is Skill?

Everyone knows that poker is a blend of skill and luck, but just how much of each ingredient is ladled into the gumbo is subject to some debate. Pros know that poker is really a long-term game. What happens today, or even this week, is too small a measure of one's skill to be meaningful. If a rank amateur were to sit down with an expert and play one hand of poker, the result would be almost all a matter of luck. If he were to play ten hands, it would still be mostly a matter of luck. If they played for hours or even played all day, short-term luck would still be strong enough to skew any results. But if the amateur and the expert were to play every day for a few months, or perhaps even a year, the distribution of cards to each player would begin to grow close to a theoretically normal distribution. In other words, once the cards come close to evening out, as they figure to in the long run, then the pro will have won much more money on his good hands and lost far less on his weak ones than his amateur opponent. At this point, the effects of short-term luck will have been bled out of the equation. The skill differential can probably be measured by the amount won by the professional and the sum lost by the amateur.

Luck Is in the Cards of the "Befolder"

Sheree recalls a time when she was late for a $500 tournament at the Taj. She quickly finished her breakfast and raced to her seat. She knew that many pros often missed the first level or two of large, long tournaments in order to keep from getting tempted into throwing in their chips too early and losing. As she arrived at her seat, she realized that she was under the gun and looked down and saw pocket aces!

What a stroke of luck, she thought! She made a raise. Another player raised behind her and a third player who had obviously won a hand before Sheree arrived raised all in! Sheree called as did player number two who had kings. The first all-in player had pocket nines.

Guess who won all the chips in that hand and probably went on to lose them in the next hour? That's right. Pocket nines hit a set. If Sheree had only taken another minute to eat her breakfast, she never would have seen the pocket aces! If Sheree hadn't gone all in. . . . Pocket aces, a blessing? Not necessarily. Sometimes a player can look down for two hours at nine-three and seven-deuce and fold hand after hand. They aren't winning pots, true, but they're also still in the tournament. Wouldn't it have been luckier for Sheree to look down at that hand and find a seven-deuce?

Well, if she were dealt 7-2 instead of a pair of aces, she'd have folded her hand and wouldn't have been eliminated from the tournament at that point, but you never know what's going to happen when you play the hands you're dealt. After all, you don't win tournaments by folding hands, and you have to take risks to have any chance of winning. And in all actuality, Sheree was no worse for the wear by being eliminated early in the tournament as compared to playing late into the event and still getting knocked out before making the money. Winning poker requires walking a fine line, and sometimes you have no control at all over what happens; occasionally, you just have to watch good hands go bad and take your lumps knowing that you'd play that hand the same way if you had to do it again.

It's Much Easier to Lose Than to Win

It's much, much easier to lose a session of poker than to win, and this is especially true when you're new to the table. The game drains your money. If ten people are sitting around the table, some are going to be great players; some are going to get lucky; some are going to stay to the river with unreasonable draws. Usually only one person gets each pot (that's one out of ten). If you don't know the other players, but they know each other, that's another huge factor that will make you more likely to lose than win.

Getting pocket aces can be good luck, but it can be the worst luck if your hand doesn't hold up and costs you a fortune! Or if it hits a set when someone else flopped a flush!

Ways to Lose Lots of Money

- Being a non-believer: A little skepticism is a healthy thing. But too much skepticism at the poker table means you're doomed to be the *table sheriff* and probably seen by your opponents as a "calling station" to boot.
- Bluffing too much: You can bluff tight, timid players all day long and half the night. But others, such as the table sheriff described above, are seldom going to fold a hand if they can help it. One of the lines separating a good from an outstanding player is the ability to differentiate between his opponents, often in the face of incomplete information. He needs to be accurate in his assessments about which players can be bluffed out of a pot, and which ones call too frequently and can be bet into for value with good hands.
- Playing too many hands: Remember the poker player's mantra. Be selective, but be aggressive. Playing too many hands violates the first part of this credo.
- Overvaluing big-card holdings: Some hands, such

as starting with K-T or K-J look a lot better than they really are. If you cold-call a raise for two bets with this kind of holding, or you come out betting and are raised by an opponent in later position, you will usually find that you're swimming upstream. It's a long, hard pull to extricate yourself from these murky waters.

- Getting married to your cards: While it's okay to fall in love with your hand, please remember that discretion is the better part of valor. You don't have to marry that hand you find yourself infatuated with. Pocket aces are beautiful pre-flop, but when the flop comes Two-Two-Five and there are two other players raising and reraising, one of them almost definitely has a deuce. The first time you fold aces may feel tragic and bittersweet, but consider it your bar mitzvah into poker adulthood. You'll be thrilled when you calculate how much you saved by throwing away big hands—even if on occasion you threw away kings and someone shows you a bluff.

Ways to Win Lots of Money

- Aggress, raise, and rarely call: While playing too passively is never the way to riches, unmitigated, maniacal aggression will lead to one thing only. You'll win a few pots early on, but once your opponents glom on to your uber-aggressive style, they'll get out of your way with most of their hands but will reraise whenever they have a good one. Because you've been raising with weaker hands, you'll be the underdog in most of these encounters.

- Know your limits: Play too small and it's some-times tough to take the game seriously. If you play for limits you can't really afford, you run the risk of putting a severe crimp in your bankroll or play-ing scared and being quickly assessed by your ad-versaries as a tight, predictable player, who will fold at the first sound of chips rattling in some-one's hand.

- Give up the little pots; win the big ones. Yes, keep grabbing the abandoned little pots, but if you're in doubt about whether you're beat and the pot is small, fold. Use your tight image to secure and nail down the large multi-way pots. In a tournament, avoid big stacks: If you go up against a big stack in a tournament, he can put you all-in. If you lose, it's bye-bye tournament, while if he loses he'll still have some weapons in hand for another battle somewhere down the line.

- Go after the tight, the timid, and the newbie: As poker expert Mike Caro says, "If they're helpless, and they can't defend themselves, you're in the right game." Poker is nothing more than social Darwinism played with cards. Show no mercy. Eat the weak.

- Take reasonable risks: Mom's old advice, "All things in moderation" works well here. Don't take unnec-essary risks and don't be overly cautious. Learning to function within these boundaries will come with practice, study, thinking about the game, and playing. It'll take time to learn this, but with time and effort it will come.

- Learn to do what comes unnaturally: Some of poker is logical, but there's a lot to the game that's just plain counterintuitive. To win some pots, you've got to bet when you have nothing but act like you've got a lot. To win others, you have to feign weakness and let your prey come to you.

- Fold big hands when you feel beat: The second-best poker hand is nothing more than the first loser. And it doesn't matter how big your hand is; if you believe your opponent has a bigger one, get out while you can still save a bet or two.

- Quit while you're ahead. Or quit while you're behind. *Stop Loss* and *Stop Win* systems are meaningless: But play when the game is good and you figure to be favored over your opponents regardless of whether you're winning now or whether you're stuck a rack or two. The game will always be there, and the decision to leave the table ought to have everything to do with the quality of the game, and precious little with whether you are currently ahead or behind.

Accounting for Your Money and Your Bankroll

"If I weren't broke, I'd be rich now," says the shocked tournament winner sleeping on his friend's couch. Most businesses that go under do so because they are either undercapitalized or have poor accounting records. Because these two hobgoblins seem to go hand-in-hand, many failed businesses have neither good accounting records—so they really don't know where their money is coming from, or, as is usually the case, where and how it's being spent—nor do they have enough money to sustain the new business through its first few, and often trying, years.

The same can be said for many failed poker players. All the pros understand and have an appreciation for how volatile poker can be. There are ups and downs and those swings can be both longer and deeper than many new players imagine.

To survive as a poker player, a sizeable bankroll is needed, and it must be carefully managed. The player who has a big win and blows most of his new money on a new car or a Rolex is setting himself up for future failure because big losses can be as common as big wins. As a professional, or even a passionate enthusiast, it is so much wiser to live below your means. As much as possible, expect to spend most of your poker winnings only on poker.

There are also a lot of myths about money management, such as whether to quit the game when you are ahead of it, or quit when you are losing. Most of these money-management systems are completely bogus. But *bankroll management*, as opposed to *money management*, is not bogus. It has serious implications for whether a player can expect to sustain him or herself given the relatively high variance that's predictable and to be expected if one chooses to play poker for a living.

Money Management

Money management is a concept that should have been buried long ago. It's a fallacious concept still making its way into gaming literature. Should you really quit while you're ahead? Should you be concerned with setting stop-loss limits and leaving the table once you've lost some pre-determined sum? Are you better off coming back tomorrow because Lady Luck cold-shouldered you, and you ought to have known better than to chase your losses?

Does this make any sense? If you quit when you're ahead, as well as when you're losing, do you only play when your results are banded between arbitrarily established stop-loss and stop-win limits?

Even money management adherents will acknowledge that a poker game never ends. If that's true, how can it make any difference if you play four hours today and four hours tomorrow, or just play eight hours today? What *is* the logic behind these money management theories?

Does It Really Make Sense to Quit While You're Ahead?

Those who believe in the *quit while you're ahead* theory say that quitting winners lets you take some profit out of the game and that it prevents giving back money you've already won. But this only makes sense if you're going to quit poker entirely. If you never play again, and you're ahead in today's game, quitting will allow you to permanently put today's profit into your pocket.

But if you quit when you're winning today and lose tomorrow, are you any worse off than if you simply played on and lost what you had won earlier in the session? Of course not. Coming back tomorrow simply allows you to pocket those winnings for a few more hours.

What About Stop-Loss Limits?

The same logic applies to *stop-loss* theory. If you are losing and leave the game, but plan to play tomorrow—or next week, for that matter—quitting makes no difference. What's important is whether you can beat the game you're playing in. If you're a favorite in that game, there's absolutely no difference between quitting now or continuing to play.

All You Need to Know About Money Management

Here's the only facet of money management that's true. If the game is good and you're a favorite, keep playing. If the game is bad and you are an underdog, quit! Never mind whether you're winning or losing.

You may be the best player in that game, but you may not be favored for any number of reasons unrelated to the relative difference between your skill level and that of your opponents. Perhaps you're tired, emotionally upset from an argument with your spouse, kids or boss, physically ill and not able to concentrate. Maybe you're stressed out from work, traffic congestion, or any other threat to the sanctity of the human condition that puts you off your game.

You can save a lot of money over the course of your poker-playing career by following this simple rule: If you're not playing up to your ability, go home. The game will still be there tomorrow.

Game Selection and Money Management

Gambling successfully is predicated on putting yourself into situations where you have a positive expectation. That's why there aren't any professional craps or roulette players. In the long run, craps players and roulette-a-holics have no chance of winning because the odds are stacked against them. You've chosen to play poker because you believe you can find games where you are favored over your opponents. While favorites do have losing nights, they also show a profit in the long run.

Since one of the key concepts to winning at any form of poker is game selection, why would you voluntarily take yourself out of a good game, simply because you have won or lost some arbitrarily predetermined amount of money? We understand that you probably want to quit if you've suffered a number of bad beats. Maybe it's one of those nights when nothing seems to be going right, even if the game is good. That's okay, but there's a difference. Now you're quitting because you're not in the right frame of mind to continue playing up to the best of your ability, not because you've reached a stop-loss limit.

What if you're in a good game and you're $1,000 ahead? Should you really quit when you're ahead? If the game is that good, and you have no other pressing commitments, why not go right on playing? After all, you're a favorite and figure to win even more money.

But whether you win or lose from that point on, those results were never predictable in advance and are always up for grabs. Keep playing or pack it in and return to the game tomorrow. It makes no difference. The game goes on, and the segments of time during which you're playing are only arbitrary delineations.

Here's all you really need to know about money management:

- As a strategy for maximizing winnings or limiting losses, money management is meaningless.
- Stop-loss limits, and quitting once you've won a pre-determined amount of money, will neither stop your losses, if you are a losing player, nor protect your profits if you're ahead.
- Poor players go broke no matter what they do. Good players establish an expected hourly win rate regardless of when they quit.
- If you're playing in a good game, and playing your best, stay in the game unless you have other obligations.
- If you're in a bad game, get out of it now—never-mind whether you're winning or not.
- If you're emotionally off kilter or otherwise not at your best, you're better off quitting, or you run the risk of your condition taking itself out on your bankroll.

Dead Money

Dead money is money that goes into the pot without much of a chance to win. The money posted by the blinds is often dead money. When a pot contains extra blinds from returning players who are posting *behind the button,* there is lots of extra dead money in the pot. Some players, particularly novices and calling stations, are unaware of what is needed to win a pot. That's why those players themselves are sometimes referred to as "dead money" by top-notch tournament players and professionals. Although novices and calling stations are capable of winning hands, most of the money they place into the pot is dead money. If you're sharp, you'll seize opportunities to collect it, and no one will be the wiser.

It's Only Money

Just before being fired, *Apprentice* contestant Alex pointed out that it's hard to hurt someone who has nothing to lose. In a cash game, or in a tournament, be very careful about isolating someone who doesn't care about chips or money. Certainly, you will not be able to bluff such a player. They'll call you, and most likely beat you, if you're on a bluff. If you have a huge stack and probably have them beat, and you make a play at them, do expect them to call with any two cards. If their winning would hurt you, then avoid them. On the other hand, your bluff or your better hand can beat anyone. Alex was fired.

Having a Lucky Night?

Look at the good player with the short stack and think, "There but for the grace of the poker gods go I." Three wrong moves and that's you.

Watch Your New Stack Grow

Here's a trick. When you start folding hands that you're aware experts don't play, such as suited high/low cards or seven/nine, pretend that you haven't folded. Now, count the money you would have saved. Similarly, when you start earning money you used to leave on the table, make a separate stack of the money you would not have earned in the past. When you start realizing that you're behind and stopped paying off the winner, especially on the river, consider the money you didn't give away as money saved. Add that to your separate stack. Now you're the winner!

Making Money Playing Poker

Although some poker players earn millions of dollars a year at the tables, most don't earn anywhere near that. In fact, the vast majority of poker players don't figure to beat the game at all in the long run, which is another way of saying that their dreams and aspirations of playing poker for a living won't bear fruit, at least not without substantial improvement.

But with the current interest in poker, more and more players—lured by the appeal of the game, its lifestyle, and television's enthusiastic coverage—hope to play professionally. Many never get around to taking the plunge. But some do. How much they earn, and whether or not they succeed well enough to earn a living at the game, depends on a wide variety of things, not all of which are related to an ability to play poker.

Obviously, an ability to play poker skillfully is a baseline requirement for success. If you can't play well, you won't earn a living at the game regardless of whatever else you might do, or whatever other personal, emotional, and intellectual attributes you possess.

Desire and Discipline

Desire and discipline are two critically important factors necessary to succeed at professional poker. If you decide to specialize in cash games for a living and are a winning player, you'll eventually establish an average amount you can expect to win for each hour you put in at the tables. It's like a baseball player's batting average. He might hit .300, but that doesn't mean he'll get three hits for each and every ten times he strides to the plate. He'll have protracted slumps that can last for a month or longer at a time, while on other occasions every time he puts the bat on the ball it will fall in for a base hit.

When you think of it that way, it makes poker's ups and downs a bit easier to take, especially when you've been keeping good records and know that any bad streak is just a blip in the data stream, and that you should figure to maintain your batting average over the course of the year. Another way to view professional poker is to analogize that it's like a job, and the more hours you put in, the more you can expect to earn. It's like being a salesperson who knows that his commission figures to increase if he puts more time in on the job.

All of this requires discipline, and discipline is as critical to a poker player as it is to a baseball player trying to hit a big-league curve ball. Without it, all the skill in the world will not be sufficient. All it takes is a short period of tilt time for an otherwise good poker player to blow back money he spent hours, days, or even weeks winning. You just can't afford to allow your discipline to take a day off when you're a working professional poker player. The price you pay if you do can be enormous.

Some pros are more skilled and more disciplined than others and they use their attributes to earn a great deal of money. Others earn very little, and while they *are* professional poker players, they're more subsistence pros than anything else. For some, it's frustrating. An inability to get their winnings up and over the hump to the point where playing poker professionally provides them with the lifestyle they seek, eventually drives them out of the game and back into a more mainstream occupation.

How Much Do You Need to Earn by Playing Poker?

Others, however, are entirely satisfied with a small wage from poker. Perhaps they don't have the same expectations or desires that other, more successful professionals have. Perhaps their poker income is merely a supplement to other income streams and they don't need to win all that much in order to live the life they desire.

With an increased interest in poker and more and more players entering the game, opportunity abounds as never before. If you are interested in earning a living at the poker table, there's probably never been a better time to give it a go than right now.

If you play cash games and you play them well, you should expect to earn approximately one big bet per hour. But that expectation is predicated on excellent play. Not good play, mind you, but outstanding poker, each and every day. One big bet per hour has always been a generally accepted notion, but no one's ever done any kind of scientific survey to validate it. Still, it seems to be a ballpark figure for most working poker pros. You can probably earn more per hour in lower-limit games, and you'll make substantially less in larger games because the players are better. On average, if you play $20–$40 or $30–$60 games for a living and you play them extremely well, you should be able to win one big bet an hour. That's $40 per hour in the $20–$40 game and $60 an hour in $30–$60 games. Whether that's sufficient to support the lifestyle you desire is a question only you can answer.

How Much Can You Expect to Earn?

You will probably earn slightly more than one big bet each hour in lower-limit games, but you might not be able to earn enough to sustain your lifestyle. At bigger limit games, such as $100–$200, don't figure on making even one big bet per hour. In fact, if you're an expert player you'll probably win more on the order of one-half to three-quarters of a bet each hour.

Is that a good living? Like most things in poker, it depends. For some folks, it's lavish; for others, it's not. These figures, by the way, are net estimates. They represent what you might expect to win after you've accounted for the rake and dealer tips. While the rake is a much larger percentage of an average-sized pot in smaller games, the playing skill of your opponents is far below what you can expect to find in bigger games. You should be able to more than compensate for it in your winnings.

Even if you're not an expert, but merely a very good player, and your earnings are half what we estimated an expert player can earn, it still might suffice. But pay attention to these caveats before you drop everything and head off to the nearest casino to make your living at the poker tables:

- If you're playing for a living at casinos that are not located in major poker centers, you will have a hard time finding games at higher limits. You might find that the biggest game in a casino near you might be $20–$40, $10–$20, or even less, and then the "big game" might not be spread on a 24/7 basis. If you don't want to move and set up shop in Las Vegas or one of the other poker Meccas, and there's not a big enough game near home to support your lifestyle, you'll have some difficult decisions to make. You'll either have to move to a locale that has big games on a regular basis, or adjust your expenditures to meet the realities of a lessened income.

- If you want to play very big games, such as $80–$160 and above, you will have to relocate to a major poker center, such as Las Vegas, Los Angeles, or Atlantic City—or else you'll have to go online to find the high-stakes games you need in cyberspace. Are there high-stakes games online? You bet. I've seen $200–$400 no-limit games on a few sites, and these are very big games indeed.

How Much Capitalization Is Sufficient to Give You a Chance of Succeeding as a Professional Poker Player?

You'll need more money than you think if you decide to play poker for a living. A bankroll that's exclusively for playing poker is your first requirement. In addition to poker money, you'll also need to sustain yourself during your first year or so as a professional player. To assure a reasonable chance of success, plan on setting aside at least 300 to 400 big bets as a poker bankroll when you're first starting out; 500 to 600 big bets provides an even better safety net. This bankroll should be used for poker only—we can't empha-size this point strongly enough—it's not for food, rent, util-ities, clothing, or your car payment. You'll need another, separate bankroll for that.

To give yourself the best chance of succeeding as a pro-fessional poker player, we recommend having twelve-to-eighteen months of expense money on hand. If you're successful, you'll reach a point at the end of a year to a year-and-a-half where you can treat some of your winnings as income. But to do that, you'll have to keep good records and establish a predictable hourly average income. From a psychological perspective, you should feel secure enough in your abilities, and in the measurable results you've achieved in your first twelve-to-eighteen months as a pro-fessional, to know that you can sustain or even exceed this level of play. Only then can you consider yourself a work-ing, professional poker player. Up until that point, you're on probation.

If these requirements seem too rigorous or overly con-servative, it's important to realize that playing poker for a living is a business and no longer an avocation. The cost of hobbies and avocations can be underwritten with money earned from other sources, usually a *day job*. When you're playing poker for a living, there is no other job to subsi-dize losses. Poker is your job and your business, too. Most new businesses that fail do so because they are under-capitalized, not because the product is inferior or the sales and marketing effort is less than adequate, or the manage-ment is poor.

When you play poker for a living, you're no different in many ways from the person starting a restaurant or open-ing up a barbershop. If you are undercapitalized, you sig-nificantly increase your risk of ruin, and why would you want to do that? We urge that you keep building your bankroll—and keep your day job, too—until you are adequately capitalized. Then give it a go. But only then, and no sooner. You'll give yourself the best chance to succeed if you do.

Financial Guidelines for Specializing in Tournament Play

If you want to play tournaments for a living, the "one big bet per hour" guideline isn't a metric that's very meaningful. Other measures apply. Many tournament players consider themselves successful if they win an average of twice the buy-in. But it takes a long time to establish an average that seems in proportion to your expectation and playing skill. The variance in tournaments is enormous. Even great, world-class players can go a year or longer without cashing in an event.

Great players have the advantage of knowing they're good, and they've proven it in the past. They know how good they are. But you won't know whether it's you or the run of cards you've been dealt when you're first cutting your teeth as a tournament specialist. At least not off the bat you won't. Until you get out and commit yourself to a poker-playing lifestyle, you have no way of demonstrating to yourself that you can beat the game, particularly when your game is tournament poker.

While a thousand hours or so will generally be sufficient to prove your ability in cash games, the fluctuations in tournament poker can go on for an even longer time. You may have to play in 1,000 tournaments before you're certain you can beat tournament poker on an ongoing basis. And if you are planning to enter tournaments with $1,000 buy-ins, take out a pencil and multiply $1,000 by

1,000. This will give you an idea of how much money you'll need—aside and apart from your living expenses—to give yourself a fair shot at proving yourself at tournament poker.

Most players don't begin their careers with a million bucks in store. It's usually a lot less than that. Some play in $100 buy-in events and work their way up from poker's minor leagues to the majors. Others have simply taken a shot at a big event, played well and were lucky right out of the box. When that happens, they have a big payday and sufficient money to pay their way into a series of big buy-in events for the next year or two.

Even that may not be enough. If they are as good as they seem, that early success will propel them to a successful career as a tournament player where they may well earn a million dollars a year or more. Others—those who were more lucky than good—may win one event and never be heard from again. They invest their winnings into other tournaments, fail to make a score, and gradually bleed themselves right off the tournament circuit. Still others have the skill but lack the discipline, and after blowing their money on a variety of other temptations, they spend their careers looking for backers to put them into big events.

Professional Poker Can Be a Hard Life

The story of legendary three-time WSOP winner Stu Ungar has been told hundreds of times. He might have been the poster child for disfunctionality in every phase of his life, except for those hours he spent at the card table. He won millions but gambled and snorted it away until he died of a drug overdose at age forty-five in a cheap, seedy, Las Vegas motel. He's not the only poker player with big-time money leaks either. His is just the most colorful and most out-rageous story in recent memory. The late Mr. Ungar is emblematic of the kinds of problems that many otherwise great players have.

Poker on the tournament circuit can be a hard life. And it's not just the extremely high variance at the poker table either. Even if you can pass life's temptations by, you have the numbing effect of constant travel, of living much of the year in hotel rooms, getting little exercise, and chowing down buffet food.

It might seem glamorous when you see it on TV, but poker can be a grind. If you're planning on playing for a living, you need to think it through very carefully before you burn your bridges and take that first step into a casino as a professional poker player.

Playing the Side Games at Tournaments

Many professionals travel the tournament circuit but never play in a tournament. Instead, they can be found in the cash games that spring up whenever there's a big tourna-ment in town. There's often the quality of a feeding frenzy created at big tournaments, and many players sit in cash games that are much larger than they are used to. In other words, while big tournaments attract some of the world's best poker players, they attract some of the biggest fish, too. In fact, some notable tournament players are notori-ously poor players when it comes to cash games. They're known to blow back all of their winnings—and then some—in the big side games that take place at tournament time.

Playing Satellites for a Living

Some players specialize in one-table satellites that spring up around major tournaments. Although satellite specialists can't expect to earn twice their buy-in, a one-table satellite takes far less time to complete. Someone who can earn a 10- or 20 percent return on his investment, and can play five satellites in one day, can do quite well. If you play in $300 buy-in satellites with a 25 percent return, each event is worth $75 to this player on average. That's a predicted win of $375 per day. Not great, but it's not bad either. If our satellite expert has that same edge in $1,000 buy-in events, he figures to win $1,250 a day, on average.

Because these satellites are only spread at major tournaments, satellite specialists also have to win at cash games too if they expect to make a good living at the poker tables.

With all of this firmly in mind, what's to prevent you from winning one big bet per hour? Absolutely nothing, but you'll have to keep working to improve your game all the time. Even if you are averaging a big bet an hour, you're not going to stop trying to improve, are you? You shouldn't. After all, your opponents are also presumably working to build up their games, and you'll have to apply the *kai-zen* concept of continuous improvement if you hope to maintain your lead over them.

How Much Money Do You Need to Play Professionally?

Here are a few things you can do to give yourself the very best chance of succeeding:

- **Prove Yourself**. You'll have to demonstrate to yourself that you can beat the game for a sufficient sum of money to live on. The actual amount depends on you. Some people can live well enough on $20 per hour. Others need twice that amount, or more. If you decide you need to generate $30 per hour to live the way you want to, then you'll have to demonstrate your ability to beat a poker game for that amount. If you can't, it won't work out for you. Trust us.

- **Beat the Game You Want to Play In**. It's one thing to beat the home game you play in every Thursday night. But if you are planning a move to Las Vegas, Southern California, Atlantic City, or any other poker Mecca where you plan to ply your skills, you need to make sure you can beat the games there. The best way to do this is to take a leave of absence from your job, or save up a month's vacation, and go. Play every day, just as you would if you were playing poker for a living. See how you do. If you can beat these games regularly, you stand a good chance of surviving and even thriving as a professional poker player.

- **Build a Bankroll**. Forget the commonly accepted wisdom. When you're starting out, be sure you err on the side of caution. If you fail because you lack the skill, that's one thing. But don't go under simply because you are undercapitalized. Instead of a 300 big-bet bankroll, begin with 400 big bets in hand. If you want to give yourself an even better chance, 500 or 600 big bets are even better. That means if you want to play $20–$40 Texas hold'em every day, you should have a poker bankroll of $24,000. A big bankroll also allows you to take shots at bigger games occasionally and, if you find you can beat those games too, you might give yourself the promotion you deserve. You won't know what to expect when you're getting started, and it makes good sense to be overfunded rather than *short-stacked*.

* **Living Expenses**. You'll need money for rent, gas for your car, food, clothing, and whatever other things you need to keep your life together. You don't want to dip into your poker bankroll for this money. If you do, you are taking the capital you need to run your business and converting it into income. When you do that, capital disappears and income is dissipated over time. You'll need to save some money over and above what you need to play on. This will allow you to keep your head above water during the first year or two you're earning your living at the poker table. You ought to figure your monthly living expenses, along with a little something to see you through those emergencies, such as a car that needs repairing or a visit to the dentist. Then multiply that monthly figure by 18 or 24 to show you what you'll need for two years' worth of living expenses, over and above your poker bankroll. If you figure it will cost $1,500 to live frugally in Las Vegas or Atlantic City each month, you'll need $36,000 in addition to your poker bankroll. We're talking about some real money here: thirty-six grand to live on and $24,000 for playing poker. In other words, to give yourself a good chance of playing and beating a $20–$40 game for a living, you should plan on a stake of $60,000. Building that kind of stake isn't easy. That's why many people wait until they re-

tire to play poker for a living. That way they have
some income coming in every month and don't
have to worry about meeting their living expenses.
They just need a bankroll for the game they plan
to play in, and they have to be able to beat it. If
you can beat the game, you'll be able to take
money out of your winnings after a while. But the
advantage of not tapping into your winnings is
that it gives you more money to climb up to the
next rung of poker's ladder.

- **Don't Burn Any Bridges**. Okay, so you've done
  all that we've suggested and are ready to give it a
  go. Do you just pack it in, tell your boss what
  you've always thought of him and the company,
  and huff on out of there? We don't recommend it.
  Take a sabbatical, if you can. Or ask for an unpaid
  leave of absence. If you do that, you might even
  convince your employer to keep you on their
  health insurance as long as you're willing to pay
  the premiums, and that can be a boon if you find
  yourself sick and in need of health care. You're off
  into uncharted waters and it may be more difficult
  than you expect. Any new venture figures to be
  fraught with inefficiencies and start-up bugaboos.
  Playing poker for a living is no different. So give
  yourself the best chance for success that you can
  muster. The only way to do that is to make certain
  that you are able to beat the game of your choos-
  ing, and that you are adequately capitalized. And
  the latter means you should have at least 400 big
  bets in one pocket and at least eighteen months
  living expenses in the other. We recommend 600
  big bets and two years' worth of living expenses,

but you probably won't listen to us. So we're hoping you go forward with at least a 400 bet bankroll and eighteen months in expenses in order to give yourself the best possible chance to make a living at this game.

6

♣ ♥

TOURNAMENT PLAY

♦ ♠

Tournament poker and ring games are as different as checkers and chess—or as different as slow-pitch softball and baseball, or touch football on the beach and playing in the NFL. The strategies required to win at each are entirely different. If you lose your stake in a cash game, you can reach into your wallet and buy more chips before the next hand. In a tournament, chips don't represent money as much as they represent a percentage of your entire equity in the event. Lose all your chips and you have no more stake in the tournament. You're eliminated. So the strategies differ.

Play is usually tighter in tournaments, with players more reluctant to call a bet because chips are precious and are not to be expended on speculative hands. That's why you will not see too many players betting with flush or straight draws in tournaments. Risking chips can be lethal to one's tournament health. But betting on a draw in a cash game, where the odds support plays like this in the long run, is good, solid, sound poker. Players who don't understand the nuances that differentiate cash game and tournament play can wind up facing problems they should have been able to avoid.

Top Tournament Strategies

Here are a few of our best tournament strategies:

- Develop a tight image early on. Once again we'd be remiss if we failed to point out that you can't win a tournament in the first few stages but you can play yourself right out of one. If you have time to craft an image at the table, establish yourself as a tight player. That will buy you a license to run a bluff through any good, observant player later on when you might really need to. Another reason for tight play in the early stages is that the cost of blinds is fairly small compared to the amount of chips in your possession. You're not yet at the point where you have relatively few chips and the blinds are large, and so you're forced to gamble with marginal hands. In the early stages, you can wait for strong hands before committing chips to the pot.
- See if you can find out how the tables will be broken down. This will give you an idea of whether or not you'll be playing with the same players for a long or short time. A tight image is more important if you are going to stay with these players. Aggression is more important if yours is the first table slated to be broken up.
- Don't make any bad calls. Notice who does make a bad call every time you make a good raise with a good hand. It's critical to scrutinize your opponents when they're involved in a hand and you're not. When you see, for example, that the guy two seats to your left will always call with any hand because he's not about to get bluffed out of a pot, you'll know to bet your good hands right into

him. But never try to steal a pot out from under his nose. Freud maintained that the third item on anyone's list is the most significant. That remains true here. If we were given only one second to tell someone how to win a tournament, the advice would be, "Don't make bad calls." If it had to be shorter than that, it would have to be culled to, "Don't call." If that is the one secret you take away from this book, with that advice alone you will come away a winning player.

- Always keep in mind that you or anyone else can raise with a hand that is far inferior to the one needed to make a good call. The corollary of this aphorism is that it takes a better hand to call with than it does to do the betting in the first place. After all, if you have a sense of the hands that someone is likely to come out betting with, you know the hands you should have to raise him. And that's usually a much smaller spectrum than the range of hands you'll feel comfortable betting.

- Notice everyone's chip stack at all times. Remember that shorter chip stacks are more desperate than larger ones and larger ones bully shorter ones. A poker tournament is like life in the wild: The strong eat the weak.

- If you're going to bully a short stack, try to get in a heads-up situation. Then you can make a bet that will force your opponent to commit all his chips to call you. No one likes to leave a tournament, especially not when they've had to call with a weak hand. But if your opponent is a short stack because he's just taken a particularly onerous beat in the last hand or two, he might just call you with any hand. He's in that kamikaze mindset of someone who is looking to double his chip count or go down in flames. There are times to steal pots and other times when you're better off just betting your good hands for value and saving your aggressive plays for another day.

- Strive to play great hands in great position. The worse the position, the stronger the hand. Don't overvalue any hand out of position. We continue to emphasize this point: Nothing succeeds like position. With good position, you are in command of the hand in a way you seldom can be when you have to act first, and cannot know either the real or purported strength of your opponent's holdings.

- Remember that every time you put any chips in the pot, your whole stack is at risk. No-limit hold'em can be a very brutal game. With all of your chips and your entire tournament life in jeopardy all the time, you'll have to prepare yourself for the inevitable: Lay down hands in a no-limit tournament that you would never consider surrendering in a fixed-limit cash game. Someday soon you'll be dealt A-K and the flop will be A-9-7. You'll bet and someone will come over the top and force you to put all or most all of your chips into the center of the pot. Although top pair with top kicker wins a lot of hold'em pots, it's a big underdog against a set of sevens, a set of nines, or two pair. Unless your opponent is a maniac or has a terrific read on you—and thereby presumes he can make you release your hand—that's precisely what he has in his hand. You're beaten, and ought to toss your big pair away. It's a sad comeuppance, but it happens. You might even be looking at a stone-cold bluff.

Nevermind. Take the safe road unless you're already so short-stacked that you need to make a stand.

- As the tournament progresses, your aggression level should progress in barely perceptible increments. You have to keep pace with the changing ration between the antes/blinds, and the size of your stack. The larger the blinds get in relation to the number of chips in your possession, the more risks you have to take to keep from being eaten alive by the escalating blinds and antes.

- Keep a tally of the number of overall chips in play and your chip stack relative to the whole. Online players can always see if their stack is high, low, or average. Live tournament players have to do math to figure this out, but it's worth it. Don't get desperate unless you really are.

- On the bubble, when the players are all about to come into the money, or at the final table, sometimes it is wisest just to sit back and let them take each other out. This is a two-edged sword. When there are only one or two players to be eliminated before all the remaining players reach the money ladder, play tends to tighten up significantly. That means an increased opportunity to steal. No one likes being eliminated immediately prior to making the money. Being the "bubble boy," or girl, is no fun. But under these circumstances there's a significant opportunity to take some calculated risks and build up your chip count without having to show down a hand. Most of your opponents, after all, are thinking just as you do: They don't want to be the last one out before the money. So play it as it lays. Decide if you feel like taking a risk under these circumstances, and then steal a few pots. Even the sheriff is usually off duty immediately before the money ladder is reached.

Rebuy Tournament Strategy

In a rebuy tournament, many players realize that the first hour is a free-for-all for maniacs and spendthrifts. They understand that the *real* tournament does not begin until after the rebuy period is over. What many players fail to realize is that the maniacs and rebuyers who are good enough to actually win the whole shebang, have a method to their madness. They are trying to get as many chips as possible at the end of the rebuy period—far more than a player can sit down and buy in for at the end of the hour with a double rebuy and an add-on. Once those players have aggressed their way into a big stack—even if that event happens only fifteen minutes into the rebuy period—they will settle down to play their *real* tournament early. In addition to understanding what they're doing, it's a good strategy that you might want to consider employing yourself—if your bankroll can stand it and if your rebuys don't cost so much that you'll need to win the tournament just to break even on your buy-in.

A Chip and a Chair

He was talking about baseball, not poker, when Yogi Berra uttered his memorable, "It ain't over till it's over" quote. But Yogi's quote is applicable to poker, too. Long before Berra uttered those memorable words, poker players always said "All it takes is a chip and a chair." And it's true. Both Jack Strauss and Linda Johnson won World Series of Poker events when down to a single chip.

They're not the only ones either. Many others have come back from very few chips to win poker tournaments or place very high in the money. The message here is simple: Never surrender. Ever. So many players suffer a bad beat in a tournament and see their chips depleted to a precious few that they give up. They usually do this by going all-in in a kamikaze-like attempt to augment their chip size, regardless of the cards they're holding. Don't do that. Instead, look for a good position to get all your chips in the center of the table. Most of the time, you should be looking for a hand where you can raise all-in instead of calling someone else's bet. And you usually want to have an ace or a pair in your hand when you make that move.

It's going to take a good deal of luck to double up, and then double up again two or three more times—until you are back and well armed with chips—but it does happen. You're much better off fighting until the bitter end than you are simply throwing away your chips because you're nearly out of ammunition. You won't get lucky all of the time. You won't come back from short-stacked situations most of the time. In fact, you'll make impossible comebacks very rarely. But rarely beats never. If you surrender because you're short-stacked and feeling down about a bad beat, you'll never make a miraculous comeback. And it doesn't take very many miraculous comebacks—one is usually enough—for your feat to become legendary and viewed as a win for the ages.

If you find yourself suddenly short-stacked, become absolutely, positively determined to win the very next pot you are in. If you do make it to the latter stages of a tournament, you can assume that most all of your opponents will be good, tricky, and aggressive because the cream usually rises to the top. And even if it doesn't, you should presume that your opponents all know how to play unless they demonstrate otherwise. And by the way, congratulations for making it this far in the tournament. We'll leave it to you to figure out how to win it.

When You've Been Raised

When you bet into a pot and are raised, you've got to rethink where you stand in the play of this hand. You probably came out betting because you believed you had the best hand and wanted to get more money in the pot. You might also have believed that you were getting the correct price from the pot and that betting a draw figured to yield a long-term positive expectation.

But now that your bet has been answered with a raise, not the call or fold that you were probably hoping for—unless, of course, you have a Goliath-sized hand and were just hoping someone would be foolish enough to raise—you've got to reassess the situation and decide what action to take based on your opponent's raise.

Here are a few questions you might want to ask yourself in this situation. It's important to bear in mind that these are not questions with right or wrong answers. Instead, you can use them as a set of interrogatories to guide you in making a decision at the table. Depending on how you interpret the data at hand, you'll fold, call, or reraise. That's it. There are only three choices to make once you've been raised. And if you are playing in a no-limit or pot-limit game—cash game or tournament, it's all the same at this juncture—and decide to reraise, you'll also have to decide how much to raise:

- How's my hand? Did I bet a big hand, a draw, or did I simply have position on my opponent and figured that betting gave me a good chance to win the pot right then and there?

- Who's in the pot with me? If you face a raise from a lone opponent who acts after you do, that's not necessarily as frightening as a raise from someone who's just seen two or three others enter the pot prior to raising. It's not so bad when someone raises after you *call* the blind. They could easily be bluffing. But you've really got to reassess your hand if someone reraises after you've raised, or one player calls, you raise, and another player reraises. Now you've got to credit them with a very strong hand. In fact, if you're in a game where players regularly bluff raise, bluff reraise, and bluff a third raise, you're either playing against a real kettle of fish or you're up against some of the toughest and trickiest players in the world. We don't think you'll find three bluff raises in a year of Sundays, and if you're prudent, you shouldn't play this hand unless you have the stone cold nuts.
- How many players are left to act? A raise from the button always smacks of a steal attempt, but a raise from early position, with a number of players still to act, usually signifies a strong hand.
- Is the prize worth the game? Pot odds—or huge implied odds, if the pot odds are not there right now—need to more than offset the odds against making your hand to make the chase worthwhile.
- Where do I stand right now? Early in a tournament, when the blinds are small in relation to your chip stack and those of your adversaries, you can refrain from calling a big raise because a loss can put you out of the tournament. But later on in the event, when the blinds have escalated and now are sizeable in relationship to your chip stack, you might have to make a stand with the hand you've

been dealt. This is especially true if folding would leave you in an extremely vulnerable position. This can be a very personal decision. If you are in a small tournament and are already in the money, you might want to call. Winning could propel you significantly higher on the pay ladder, while folding in hopes of inching your way up the ladder one rung at a time might only garner another $20 or $30. But if you're in the main event at the World Series of Poker and the next notch on the pay ladder is worth an additional half million dollars, you might decide to fold and hope a very short-stacked opponent will bust out on his blinds, thus increasing your payday significantly.

Knocked Out with Kings: Why Does It Always Happen to Me?

Getting knocked out of a tournament with a pocket pair of kings seems to be the particular bugaboo of many players. They hate it. And we understand why. Pocket kings are a big hand, and no one likes losing when they are heavily favored from the get-go. Whenever it happens, it's memorable; that's for sure. When you are eliminated from a tournament or severely crippled and would have been KO'd if your opponent had a sufficient amount of chips to cover you, you can rest assured that it will happen with your good hands, not your weak ones. You're just not going to get eliminated with hands like 8-3 offsuit except for those occasions when you go all-in on your blind and that horrid 8-3 was the random hand you happened to be dealt.

When you make big bets before the flop, it's usually going to be with a significantly sized hand. Since a pocket pair of aces wins a lot more than a pocket pair of kings, it's

the KO with kings that seems most memorable. Even elimination with Big Slick doesn't stick in your memory to the
same extent, because as good as it is, A-K is still a drawing
hand and an underdog to any pair at all in a heads-up confrontation. But things are different when you're holding a
pair of kings in the pocket. You're favored against any other
holding except a pair of aces, and if you have pocket kings
and your opponent has A-K, you're still favored since he is
essentially drawing to only three outs—oddball straights
and four-card flushes notwithstanding.

An opponent figures to hold a pocket pair of aces when
you have a pocket pair of kings very infrequently. Since you
figure to have a pair of kings about once every 220 hands,
you probably won't be involved in an aces-versus-kings pre-
flop match-up very often, which is why it seems so devastating when it does.

Just don't waste time or energy worrying about situations like these. You don't get dealt big pocket pairs all that
frequently, and when you do, you're going to have to risk
your money if you want to propel yourself up the tournament leader board.

On the other hand, if you raise with a pocket pair of
kings and see an ace flop, it's an entirely different story.
With an ace in his hand, your opponent figures to pair it
on the flop one time in six, and that's not all that uncommon.

Calling

Calling can be dangerous. Not only that, when you call a
bet on the flop or turn in a no-limit game—tournament or
cash game, it makes no difference—you invite your opponent to make an even bigger bet on the turn or river. If the

cost of calling a bet is 15 percent of your stack on the flop, you run the risk of facing a bet for anywhere from 30 percent of your chips to all of them on subsequent betting rounds. So, while calling a bet in a no-limit game might serve to close out the betting for that round, it allows your opponent to fire at you with even bigger guns on the next round or two. That's why calling is not the best of ideas in a no-limit game, unless you have a draw to the nut straight or nut flush, and can see the next card inexpensively. But if you don't have a hand that can grow into the best hand, you can find yourself either making a very weak call for most or all of your chips, or else you're likely to find yourself priced out of the hand by a big bet on the next round.

Check-calling the flop in early position, then betting the turn, is a ploy many pros use. But it's not used very often by recreational players, and when it is, it's a clue that the turn card really helped them. Many professional players will call a bet on a ragged flop, and then come out betting if a big card appears on the turn. This play forces the pro's opponent to rethink the strength of his hand. After all, the pro might have called a flop of 9-5-3 with two overcards, such as Q-J. When a queen is dealt on the turn, the natural reaction of anyone holding another queen is to come out betting. So the pro, even though he might be holding nothing more dangerous than J-T, will represent a newly minted top pair by betting the turn. If his opponent was bluffing into the flop, he will almost surely release his hand, unless the turn card also gave him a draw to go along with his bluff. This play works quite well against a player who fancies himself disciplined enough to release a hand whenever it appears that his opponent has made a better hand than he has.

Where's the Tipping Point?

Although it varies from table to table and player to player, as well as from hand to hand, you still need to pay attention to the amount of a raise that tends to cause your opponents to fold marginal and good-but-not great hands. Many tables seem to develop standard-sized raises, although these will vary in size as the blinds increase and when antes are put into play along with the blinds. But if you can pin down that amount, or even a range of amounts, you'll be able to determine how much to bet if you want to chase players out of the pot, or the upper limits of some smaller amount that will encourage your opponents to call.

If you examine this from a purely theoretical perspective, you'd like to know the maximum price you can charge your opponent to extract a call with your good hands, as well as the minimum you will have to wager in order to drive them all out of the pot. Those amounts can be fairly close, or they can be very far apart. You'll never know with complete certainty, but it's one of those things you'll have to get a sense of in order to raise in the most effective and efficient manner.

A Good Tournament Bluff

In a no-limit tournament, when you see a player consistently raising her good hands with the same amount, say $200, and you feel reasonably sure that this player doesn't bluff with that particular amount, try to create an opportunity when no one else is in the pot to trick her into folding. If you bluff with a $200 bet, you'll be waving her own favorite weapon in her face, and she's likely to fold all but her very best hands.

Negating Positional Disadvantage

Suppose you're in either the small or big blind in a tournament with $4,000 in chips. Then one of your opponents with $1,000 remaining raises the $150 big blind $300. You look down at your hand to find A-K, a good hand but one that's still vulnerable to any pocket pair. If you call, you're letting your opponent have a look at the flop, and you'll find yourself in the unenviable position of having to act before him on each subsequent betting round.

If you reraise another $300 and he calls, he's going to be very short stacked and committed to the pot in any event. But if you reraise and put him all-in in the process, you accomplish two things: First, you put him to the test. He's now forced to make a decision that will cost him his tournament life if he calls and loses. Second, by putting him all-in, you've negated whatever positional advantage he'll have on succeeding rounds. Once you or your opponent is all-in, there's no advantage to being first or last on any subsequent betting round. Each of you will get to see all five community cards and when a hand goes to a showdown, position in the betting order is irrelevant.

The Object of Your Desire

One point worth bearing in mind is that in tournaments not every player has the same objectives. While every player wants to win, some are really more interested in playing conservatively toward the end in order to ensure they make it onto the pay ladder. Others are willing to take risks in order to move as far up the pay ladder as possible, because in most tournaments, the big money goes to the first three finishers. While finishing in tenth, or twentieth place guarantees that you'll win some money, it's not nearly as much as the first place finisher. That might not make much difference to the average player at the World Series of Poker's main event. Just making the final table there guarantees that you'll walk away with a life changing sum of money. But run-of-the-mill, everyday kinds of tournaments—the kind you'll find at your neighborhood casino—are not like that at all. In these smaller tourneys, coming in toward the bottom of the pay ladder usually doesn't bring much of a payday at all.

How to Play the Small Stack

When you get to the final table, or in a one-table satellite, you have to gradually increase your aggression and be very aware at every moment of your position. Be especially wary of calling anything. Be aggressive with the button or any ace or any king. Just be willing to fold to anyone who is willing to go over the top all-in if you don't have the nuts. When you are short stacked, which by definition is when you have less than ten times the big blind, you *must* go all-in if you intend to play a hand. Do not call. Do not raise less than all of your chips. If you decide to play when you are short stacked, you must be prepared to risk your entire tournament life.

When you're a short stack, opponents with a lot of chips can't get hurt by calling and losing to you. So you must fire all the ammunition at your disposal, and that's every chip in front of you. If you lose you'll be out of the tournament. If you win, you'll have *doubled through* and have twice the chips you had before the hand started.

If risking your entire tournament life seems like radical therapy, it is. But sometimes you have no other option available to you. Once you're painted into a corner, drastic steps are required to escape, and if you're going to die, at least you should die well. It's a lot better to go down firing all your guns than to whimper your way out of existence on some hopeless hand.

Bubblectable

Play slows down when everyone is waiting for three, two, or one more person to be eliminated from an event. Once those players are eliminated, all the remaining players will finish somewhere in the money. If you are willing to be the last person eliminated from the event—it's called *going out on the bubble*—you stand a good chance of stealing quite a few blinds. Many players, particularly those who are short stacked and are just hoping to finish anywhere in the money, will fold most of their hands. They want the others to be eliminated first. They want to ensure themselves a payday. These players have given you a license to rob them blind. If you are willing to take some risks—and those risks are certainly smaller than they are when players are actively engaged in a normal game—you can gather quite a few chips during these periods.

Another time where you'll find extraordinary tight play is during events that are on TV. Most often, only the final table will is televised, and it's often only the top six players who get to mug for the camera. Since most players want face time before a national TV audience, a very slow period occurs immediately prior to establishing the final table, or the final six, or however many competitors will play for the cameras. This is another great chance for the risk taker—or the person who simply doesn't care whether he appears on television or not—to steal a few blinds and put himself in better chip position.

The Long Odds in Tournament Poker

While everyone wants to win the main event at the World Series of Poker, the odds are, to say the least, against it. With fields of 6,000, everyone is a long shot, regardless of how good he or she might be. That number is staggering just on the surface, but when you begin to dig into it, it becomes even more amazing. It's particularly interesting when you think about handicapping the event and begin analyzing what kind of chance any single player has of beating a field that large.

Let's take a good player. No, make it a great player. Make him the greatest hold'em player who ever lived. Suppose his chances are ten times greater than those of Joe Average, even though the chasm between great and average is probably not anywhere near that deep. With that kind of edge, our hero figures to win a 6,000 player event once every six-hundred times. If he has a 60-year poker-playing career, he ought to win the World Series of Poker once every ten life-times. An average player, by comparison, figures to win all the marbles only once in a hundred lifetimes, and we don't know anyone whose karma will bring them back that many times.

No one can ever really be *favored* to win an event with 6,000 entrants. But someone will. Someone wins the lottery every week, and those odds are a lot longer than 6,000-to-1. Someone will play extremely well, have inordinately good luck, and go on to win this event. Since good luck includes the absence of bad luck—and precludes ridiculously bad beats—getting through a 6,000 player field probably requires placing a premium on surviving the first few days of the event. This is more important than aggressively going after chips early on. After all, if you find yourself going all-in too many times, you figure to be outdrawn some of the time. Too many draw outs can put a severe crimp in your once-in-ten-lifetime chance of winning.

When you think about it this way, you can laugh at players who tell you they are going to win the event this particular year because of the great poker they're playing, or because they feel extremely lucky. Neither statement stands up to the numbers, and unless these overconfident poker players figure to live six hundred years or longer, they can't even claim to be a favorite within their own lifetime. This sort of thing makes Dan Harrington's win in 1995 coupled with his recent spate of final table finishes all the more amazing. It's testimony to his incredible skill as well as the validity of "Action Dan's" playing style. He has the ability to continue to survive and to avoid putting all his chips at risk until he gets close enough to sniff the money.

When the Most Significant Factor Is the Money

In a tournament, great players will usually make their betting decisions based on their opponents' stack sizes. Usually they only want to play against shorter stacks. Typically, they will make a bet or a raise that would cut a big dent—either a quarter or a half—into the opponent's net worth, if called. The opponent then must make a move over the top of the aggressor's bet, often putting himself all in, which he's not likely to do without an enormous hand. Of course, the aggressor is counting on the fact that the odds of this particular short stack having kings or aces are slim at this particular moment. If that player is brave enough to go over the top all-in, then the aggressor will release this particular hand and try again on the next round.

Tournament Money

Short stacks are always looking to *double up*, and tall stacks are always looking to *vacuum up*. When you're in a tournament and the blinds have increased, but your stack of chips has dwindled, you might find yourself *short-stacked*. The generally accepted definition of short-stacked is when you have no more than ten times the big blind in your possession. You might have begun the tournament with $1,500 chips and blinds of $5-$10, but after a few hours you might find yourself with only $900 in chips and blinds of $50-$100.

You're short-stacked, and that's going to have a big impact on how you play. For starters, you no longer have the discretion of playing drawing hands, or speculative holdings, such as 9-8 suited. If you play them and don't connect, you run the risk of exiting the tournament with a hand that can't even beat a pair of deuces, or even a hand like king-high.

Short-Stacked Players Must Bet All Their Chips, If They Bet at All

Whenever you have a hand worth betting, you must commit all your chips to the center of the table. A less-than-all-in bet is not going to scare anybody out of the pot. You're no danger to any of your more well-heeled opponents, and they will call with any hand that has the proverbial snowball's chance of beating yours, unless you're willing to bet a sizeable portion of chips. And in your case, that's all of them.

That's a very different situation from earlier in the tournament. Then you could bet three or four times the big blind and if someone made a large reraise, you could fold all but your very best hands. But now you don't have that option. Your tournament life is in danger every time you make a play at the pot. And if you refrain from making a play at the pot, you'll simply hemorrhage your tournament life right down the drain.

When you're circling the drain, you need to double up. That means getting all your chips in the center of the table, hope you're called, and pray that you win the confrontation. Now you'll have twice what you did when the hand began, and you've doubled up. If you're really fortunate, you might even triple up. But in any event, you had to risk your tournament existence to do this, and that's just not something the big stacks usually worry about.

If you've been able to build a large stack of chips during the course of the event, you'll probably be content to chip away at your opponents, attack the short stacks—who can't defend themselves very readily—and add to your stash of chips incrementally. If you do go all-in, you want to do so when you have a huge edge on your opponent. That's usually after the flop, when you've made something like top set, or the nut straight or nut flush and get action from someone else who thinks he's got your number. Now doubling up can make you one of the tournament leaders, but regardless of how nice that feels, your intention is more often centered around small, slow, sure, progressive stack augmentation.

Note that some people will try to isolate the maniac. This can work or prove costly. Do so yourself when you have an enormous hand. In a tournament, try not to put your big stack at risk against him. Use him to double up your short stack.

7

ONLINE PLAY

Two things have contributed to poker's remarkable growth in recent years. One is the advent of the small "lipstick" camera that enables TV viewers to see what the players cannot: each player's hole cards. In so doing, it created viewing interest in the game and made it a staple of TV programming. The other growth element is online poker.

We can't give you any advice that will advance your dreams of becoming a TV star, but we can provide you with information about online poker, and how it differs from the game you find in a traditional, brick-and-mortar casino.

Both of your authors are ardent online players, and while poker is poker, the very nature of the Internet makes for some unique differences. In addition, you can find a game or poker tournament online twenty-four hours a day, seven days a week. Because games are faster online—dealers don't have to make change or manually shuffle the cards, and players can involve themselves in two, three, four, or more games simultaneously—you can get more practice in a week of online play than in a month of casino play. It's no wonder many of the nascent superstars of poker learned their game online. They can play more, practice more, and learn more in a relatively short period of time. So can you.

Experts Won't Tell You Why Online Players Are Doing So Well Because Their Egos Are Too Big

Most experts have big egos, and until the recent spurt in poker's popularity, it was a fairly small fraternity of players, especially at the upper levels of the game. That's all changed and the tournament poker world is full of players no one ever heard of three years ago, and they are winning events with regularity. "So who are these unknowns that are coming out of the woodwork, and why are they winning?" the long-time pro might ask himself.

The online players, located everywhere and anywhere in the world, have some unique tools at their disposal that players who honed their skills exclusively in traditional land-based casinos do not have. When you play online, you have access to as many tournaments as you'd like to play. It's possible to get a year's worth of experience online in as little as a month, and many of these new online players have climbed the learning curve quite rapidly. When they finally enter a big land-based event and do well, they're seen as *Internet players* who just got lucky. In reality, they were sequestered online, out of sight of anyone that might sit up and take notice, honing their skills to a fine edge in a relatively short period of time.

Take Note of Taking Notes

Online players make up for in *notes* what they lack in *tells*. Most of the online programs allow players to take notes about their opponents. Sheree, who used her copious notes

to win a seat at the World Series of Poker for $33, by plac-
ing first in a field of 433 will attest most strenuously to the
power of notes. Online, Sheree found that most players
were consistent in the size, strength, and frequency of their
bets, raises, bluffs, and calls. Notes are so much more useful
and reliable than tells, which are now so widely known
that they are frequently hidden or misread. Sheree was also
able to tell where she stood in the tournament at every moment and was pleased to see that she remained in first
place for 70 percent of the tournament. In person, it's impossible to know while you're playing if someone at another table is dominating the field or winning and losing
mountains of chips. This is important information when
you're strategizing about how to win a tournament. Thus,
it is no surprise that online players were shining so brightly
at the recent World Series of Poker final tables.

Taking notes when playing online is the only way to
keep track of players. In traditional brick and-mortar casinos, where you're face-to-face with the opposition, your
opponent's facial characteristics will allow you to remember how he plays and what his style is like. But when you're
online and all you have to look at is an inanimate "avatar"
instead of a player, it's tough to impossible to associate
playing characteristics with that two-dimensional picture,
particularly when you might not have played with that opponent for a month or more. But notes are accurate, much
more so than memory. They enable you to recall that a particular opponent was the player who cold-called three bets
with J-9 off-suit and stayed all the way to the river only to
lose to a bigger hand. Notes will tell you who's loose and
who's tight, and who is passive and which players are aggressive.

Closely related to note taking online is the stats function. It's your built-in reality check on exactly how disci-

plined a game you're playing. It allows you to see the hands you've played during a session, how often you've called the flop, what percentage of hands you've won when you called the flop or stayed to the river, or which betting round you've folded on most often.

Statistics don't lie; they tell the real story of your online performance. If you're losing, examining your stats will show whether your game is slipping or whether you've just experienced a bad run of luck. Your stats also provide you with valuable information during tournaments.

Keep the Tournament Lobby Open
Beside the Playing Table

Keep your eye on the lobby or, if that's not an option on a given site, you should at least be able to click on the Lobby function to see how many players remain. You can view the leader board to see where you stand in relation to your competition. It's especially important to note how many players need to be eliminated before you reach the money. In traditional tournaments, when players get close to the money, you'll often see players popping up like prairie dogs between hands to wander around the room, looking at the chip stacks of their opponents who are playing on other ta-bles. Chip and position reckoning is not an easy task in a traditional casino, and it's impossible to do accurately. But online, all you have to do is glance at the lobby and some statistical functions. You'll be provided with an accurate picture of where you stand in relation to your opponents and the money ladder. Watch the top spot. See who the leader is. Note if that person is volatile or is holding the top. Then you'll know if the leader is a stable player or someone who just makes lots of aggressive plays. That information will help you when you get to the final table.

Double Agents

Many online players are fond of playing two, three, and sometimes four or more games simultaneously. When you're actively involved in that many hands, it's impossible to take notes and concentrate on a multitude of games simultaneously. Opponents who play multiple games are playing suboptimal poker. They haven't the time to take or refer to their notes, and they can't get a feel for the texture of the game when they're jumping around from table to table. If you see an opponent who appears to be playing in a few games simultaneously—perhaps you've noticed that he takes an inordinate amount of time to make even the simplest and most obvious of decisions—you can validate this by using the site's software to locate that particular player.

If you do find that he's playing two or more games simultaneously, and taking more time than expected to make decisions in your game, take it for a given that he's playing *A-B-C poker* and has neither the time nor the ability to maneuver adeptly through the subtleties and nuances of a multiplicity of games. Chances are he's folding bad hands and raising with good ones. Respond accordingly.

One of the things that's *tres cool* about playing online poker is the opportunity to play as many games as you and your computer can accommodate. Many online poker devotees now have two or more monitors hooked together and can scroll between them, thus allowing them to play four or more games simultaneously without having to keep bringing different game screens to the foreground.

But playing in two or more games simultaneously is a double-edged sword. If you are a good player, even though you figure to play less than your best when forced to divide your attention among a couple of games, the overall amount you figure to win will increase, as long as your win rate at two tables is more than half of your normal win rate at one.

If you play at four tables simultaneously and can beat those games, you have an even bigger edge. Suppose you can beat one game for $28 an hour. If you play four games, all you have to do is beat them for more than $7.00 per hour for your overall win to increase. If you can beat four games for an average of $10 per hour each, you'll win $40 per hour overall, and that's a lot better than the larger win of $28 per hour you were able to achieve at one table.

On the other hand, if you're a losing player, or even a small winner, be careful. Playing more than one game at once can tip you over that line separating long-term winners from perennial losers, and you will lose more money by playing more games.

If you're on a short bankroll, playing at more tables can also be beneficial. It will allow you to drop down in limits, play in games that are probably easier to beat, and win the same amount as you might win playing at a single high limit table with less risk.

It Takes Time to Earn Respect

In tournaments, players get moved. Whether you're playing online or in a brick-and-mortar card room, if you stay in the tournament long enough, you'll see a new player at your tournament table. Often players who are moved are slightly tilting and discombobulated. They don't take time to feel out the new table. They assume whatever image they had at the old table has magically carried over with them. Take advantage of this phenomenon. Start to assess this new player immediately by gauging his chip stack. If it's big, try to determine whether he got those chips by waiting for excellent hands and doubling up or by playing many hands aggressively. If he's short-stacked, try to take his emotional temperature. Did he just take a big hit at the other table? Is he desperate to play too many hands now? Does he think if he sits down and raises everyone will fold?

If you're moved to a new table in a tournament, take time to assess the table and develop a new image. You're going to have to earn respect all over again, which you should see as a welcome challenge.

Online Tells

Online poker *action prompts* provide split-second efficiency, and make it impossible to act out of turn. As a consequence, your opponents will never know what you've done, or what you plan to do, before you take action or time out.

Although acting out of turn is impossible in a cyber poker game, you can direct the game's software to execute your action for you. In other words, you can make your decision, tell the computer what to do via a single mouse click, and your decision will be executed as soon as possible *without playing out of turn*. Pre-action check boxes automate your specified choice—you can check or bet, or fold, call, or raise—at the very moment the action reaches your seat. The other players will know only that you acted quickly and decisively in turn.

By making wise use of pre-action checkboxes, it's easy to play in another game at the same time, or you can read, watch TV, or do a dozen other things while playing. Pre-action checkboxes also assist in picking up tells (or false tells) when someone acts very quickly. For example, after a player has bet, if the next player raises in a split-second, he probably used the "bet or raise" or "raise any" checkbox. This usually signifies a powerful hand, but it could also be a deceptive maneuver. How can you tell for sure? It's not easy. Because no tell is 100 percent certain, the answer lies in keeping good notes on your opponents. Some players always delay a very long time before raising with a strong hand. Others will designate their raises in advance. Tells online are like those in traditional games: They have to be viewed against your own knowledge of each opponent's playing proclivities.

Online chatting, or the cessation of all dialogue by a player who had been prattling on for the past few minutes, often offers strong clues about the strength of someone's hand. When someone abruptly stops chatting, he is either pondering a close decision, or sitting back thinking about how best to get the most money out of his powerhouse hand.

Taking notes helps you keep this all straight. We can't emphasize enough how taking notes is one of the most valuable features found online—and one of the easiest to use. Used in conjunction with a player's timing delays and use of the pre-action check boxes, notes are the best way to document and decipher online tells.

Playing High-Speed and Short-Handed Games

The ability to play in multiple games is increased if you avoid the turbo, or high-speed games, and the short-handed games often found online. These games require quicker action and offer less thinking time for players. If you can react at lightning speed and make good decisions while you're playing, online poker might prove to be your cup of tea.

The disadvantage of playing many games simultaneously is that it is tougher to concentrate. Players come and go quickly. One of your best weapons, the ability to take, retain, and access notes on your opponents is severely limited

by time unless you are one of the world's great speed typ-
ists. In a brick-and-mortar casino, it's possible to see a
player you last played against five or six months ago and
recall his tendencies and how he plays. But online, it's
tough to recall screen names, and there are no mannerisms
to serve as a memory pump. Notes are your one best source
of keeping a book on your opponents. If you are playing so
many games simultaneously that you find it impossible to
take notes, you are surrendering quite a bit of edge.

While there's probably more to be gained from playing
two or more games simultaneously online, we'd recommend that you not play in so many that you can no longer
take notes on your opponents. If you are a good player and
can beat online games, then feel free to play as many as
you can handle—but record your impressions of your opponent's play.

It's a compromise, to be sure. More games usually results in less money won in each game, but the idea is not
your win per table. If you can reach a point where you are
able to beat more games for a greater total win than you
could expect to win at one table, and you are still able to
take notes about your adversaries, you've reached your optimal playing zone.

Statistical Evidence

When playing online you have another weapon at your
disposal. You can use software to garner stats that will tell
you, for example, how often you called before the flop. It will
also tell you how many hands you won at the showdown,
as well as the number of pots won without a showdown.
All of these statistics are clues to your own play. And while
they may vary from day to day, simply by virtue of whether
you are getting better or poorer starting hands, over the

long haul your playing percentages will give you a very good idea about whether you are playing too many pots, too few of them, or are continuing to call when all hope is gone.

Statistics provide a built-in reality check on how well you're playing. To view stats about how many hands you've played in a session, how often you've called the flop, the percentage of hands won when calling the flop or staying to the river, just click on the icon for stats. They don't lie. And they don't permit any self-deception either. They tell the real story of your online performance. Examine them during each playing session to determine how you might improve. Do your stats change after you've lost a few big hands or if you've played too many hours? You won't know unless you look.

What's Going On Here?

When you're competing in an online tournament and you're suddenly moved to a new table, there is a distinct advantage available to you that doesn't exist in a live tournament. Most players probably fail to take advantage of it. At a brand-new table, you have the luxury of scrolling back and seeing what has transpired before your arrival. Find out who won the pots and with what kind of hands. What have the players been saying to each other? This information can be very valuable to you, the new kid on the block.

8

MINIMAL MATH

Mathematics and poker have a funny relationship. Poker is bounded by statistical and mathematical parameters. Even if you don't understand the underlying numbers, your chances of completing a flush whenever you start with two suited cards and two more of your suit appear on the flop, are the same regardless of whether or not you can do the math.

But math isn't all there is to poker. Not by a long shot. If it was, all the best players would be mathematicians or statisticians, and they're not. Nevertheless, all of the best players understand poker's underlying mathematical precepts even if they can't do the calculations themselves. They know the odds against making their hand and understand the relationship between that and the size of the pot.

So should you. This chapter is not designed to teach you all there is to know about poker mathematics and statistics, but it will give you some simple methods for working out the more commonly encountered relationships yourself. If you can handle the numbers, you'll find yourself light-years ahead of your competition in understanding poker's underlying mathematical and statistical concepts. Even if you can't do the calcs, we've provided a chart depicting the basic odds that cover the vast majority of recurring hold'em situations.

What Are My Odds of Winning?

If you watch televised poker, you'll always see the show's expert commentators quote the odds of the opponents' hands whenever one player goes all-in. How do they do it? Are they mathematical wizards who quickly do the calculations while the hand is going on? Do they use a computer to figure the odds while the hand is in progress and record their commentary during post-production?

They probably don't do either. Instead, they've memorized the odds for common situations that arise whenever an opponent puts you all-in. You can learn these odds, too, and when you do, you'll have the same information at your disposal that the pros do. After all, knowledge is power and while poker is a game of incomplete information, having the odds at hand allows you to make more informed decisions at the poker table.

A Short Course in Pot Odds

No matter how you slice it, poker always revolves around this primary relationship: Does the pot offer enough money—or promise to offer enough money once all the betting rounds are concluded—to overcome the odds against making your hand? You can't escape it. The relationship between the pot's size and your chances of making the winning hand threads its way through every form of poker you might play.

It winds its way though real life, too. "Is the prize worth the game?" This question encapsulates the essence of decision-making at the poker table and in the real world, too. In real life, the answer always depends, since everyone's personal equation for relating the cost of an item to its personal value differs. But poker metrics are less subjective, and one has the advantage of being able to count the pot, calculate the odds against making a hand, and decide whether to fold, bet, call, or raise.

That's the very reason poker is a game you can beat, and it's why good players beat poor players in the long run. If you're shooting dice, each and every bet—from the bad ones, like hardways and the yo bet, to better wagers, like betting the pass line and taking the odds—carries a negative expectation. No system yet devised enables you to package a group of individual bets with negative expectations and rewrap them into a magic parcel of wagers that will pay off in the long run.

Poker is beatable, in part, because the odds are not immutable; they shift and change as each card is dealt from the deck. In some games, like 7-card stud, figuring the precise odds against making your hand can be difficult. This is especially true in the heat of battle, because calculations change with each card dealt on every betting round. You may start out with three hearts in your hand and not see another heart in any of your opponents' exposed upcards. But on the next round of betting, four of your opponents might be dealt a heart, and that dramatically changes your hand's risk-reward ratio. After all, there are only thirteen cards of each suit in a deck. You have three and need two more to complete your flush. Each heart dealt to an opponent is one that will never find its way into your hand. You don't need to know much about poker or probability to realize that you stand a much better chance of receiving a heart when ten of them remain in the deck instead of six—and, in this case, you still need two of them.

It's a bit easier to figure the odds in hold'em, because there are only so many situations to be accounted for, and far fewer exposed cards to consider. If you work out the relationships in advance by memorizing the odds against making particular hands in commonly encountered situations—like flopping four to a flush or four to a straight—half of your work is already done. All that remains is counting the pot.

Michael Wiesenberg, in *The Official Dictionary of Poker*, defines pot odds as: "The ratio of the size of the pot to the size of the bet a player must call to continue in the pot." For example, if the pot contains $20 and you must call a four-dollar bet, you are getting pot odds of 5-to-1.

If there are no more cards to come, and no players remain to act after you, then all you need do is consider the pot odds. If your chances of winning are better than the odds the pot is offering you, it pays to call. Otherwise you should fold—unless you think a raise will cause your opponent to release his hand, in which case that's the preferred action. But let's ignore the impact of bluffing for a moment and focus our attention on the relationship between pot odds and the chances of making your hand. If you figure to win once in three times when the pot is offering you 5-to-1 odds, it pays to call, regardless of whether you win this particular hand or not. It's the long run that matters in poker, not the outcome of any given hand.

But on earlier betting rounds, when there are still more cards to be dealt, it's difficult to know with any degree of precision how much it will cost to try and make your hand. At this point, you can never be sure how the betting will proceed or how many opponents will stick around and pay you off if you make the winning hand.

Implied Odds

That's where implied odds come into play. *The Official Dictionary of Poker* defines implied odds as, "The ratio of what you should win—including money likely to be bet in subsequent rounds—on a particular hand to what the current bet costs." Calculating implied odds is imprecise and really a form of reckoning at best, since one never knows how many opponents will remain in the hunt, or how much money will be wagered on subsequent betting rounds.

The more betting rounds in a particular game—all else being equal—the bigger the role played by implied odds. In games like draw poker or lowball, with only two rounds of betting, implied odds are not as significant as they are in hold'em, which has four betting rounds, or 7-card stud, which has five.

Implied odds are affected by a number of factors. They're better whenever your hand is hidden because your opponents might not realize what you're holding. So, they'll pay you off when they have inferior hands. If you're playing 7-card stud, you might have four unsuited, unrelated cards exposed on your board, and have a full house or even four of a kind. A hidden hand begets much higher implied odds than a hand that shouts out its strength for the entire world to see.

Suppose four jacks are exposed in your 7-card stud hand. Your implied odds are pretty much zilch, zero, nada, nil, and nothing at that point. Unless your opponent can beat four jacks, he's going to take his hand and toss it away. He can't beat you, he can't bluff you, and he won't pay you off either.

Betting structures affect implied odds too. When betting limits double on later rounds, implied odds increase. Since your opponent may call a bet on later rounds because of pot size alone, that extra bet increases the implied odds. Your opponents, just by virtue of their playing style, can increase or reduce implied odds. Players who seldom bet or raise but call to the bitter end, increase implied odds because you can draw to your hand on the cheap, knowing all the while you'll get paid off if you make your hand.

Implied Odds Are Always Greater in Pot-Limit or No-Limit Games

If you're playing no-limit or pot-limit poker, as opposed to games with fixed betting limits, the implied odds can be immense, because you can wager large amounts of money into relatively smallish pots. That's why you'll sometimes see top pros take the flop in televised no-limit games with hands they would throw away in fixed limit games. If they can see the flop for one bet, even with weak, long-shot hands such as A-4 suited or T-7 suited, they will then see five sevenths, or 71 percent, of their hand, for the cost of one bet. And if they are lucky enough for the flop to hit them twice, or better yet, give them a straight or a flush, the implied odds more than overcome all the other times when they took the flop only to release their woefully weak hand when the flop did not help them.

If you're last to act, regardless of whether you're in a fixed-, pot-, or no-limit game, you can take advantage of what your opponents have done to increase your implied odds. But players who have the ability to discern what kind of hand you're holding, even if they don't have the advantage of seeing exposed cards, will reduce your implied odds as long as they have the discipline to release their hand once they know they are beaten.

Acting first seldom helps your implied odds. Whenever you act first, it's a guessing game of sorts. You never really know whether a wager will cause opponents to fold or if they'll play back at you by raising. When forced to act before your opponents, their actions can reduce the odds you're getting to draw for your hand.

There's another concept that comes into play, too, and that's the amount of money already in the pot. That money is the reason you might want to continue to play a hand even though you are not the favorite. Here's an example: If you flop a four-flush playing hold'em, the odds are 1.86-to-1 against completing your hand. In addition, there's always the chance that you might make your flush but lose to a bigger hand. Even though you are not favored to win the hand, you might be a *money favorite*. In other words, although you might win the pot just once every three times you find yourself in that situation, it pays to draw as long as the pot promises to return two dollars or more for each dollar you have to pay to draw to your flush.

Here's another example, and as absurd as it may seem, it makes it easy to illustrate the point about being a money favorite while not an outright favorite to win the pot. Suppose a wealthy eccentric is running around your favorite card room randomly tossing five-thousand dollar chips into pots. Let's assume you flopped a flush draw in a $20–$40 hold'em game against only one opponent, and you know with absolute certainty your opponent has flopped a set of kings. Normally the relationship between the pot odds and the odds against making your hand would suggest that you fold. But with an additional $5,000 in the pot, you should call all bets until the bitter end.

After all, with three rounds of betting to go, you can lose a maximum of $20, $40, and $40 on each betting round. You don't even have to call that last bet on the river if you fail to make your hand, since you know your opponent has you beaten unless you make your flush and the board fails to pair. Since you stand to win substantially more than the cost of a couple of bets, this is not the time to save a buck by folding. While I've never played a hand of poker where the relationship between the pot odds and odds against making my hand were that good, the fact remains that the amount of money currently in the pot is the third force to be reckoned with when considering pot odds and implied odds.

Suppose you knew you were a 4-to-1 underdog in a situation like this. And to make matters worse, let's assume the pot is capped on each betting round. That's a cost to you of $80 before the flop, $80 on the flop, and $160 on the turn. We won't count the river because you will always fold unless you make your flush. Your cost to play each hand is $320. If you figure to win once in every five confrontations, in the long run you'll lose $320 four times (for a total of $1,280). But when you win, you'll gather in the additional $5,000 that's been added to the pot plus all the bets there. In the long run, when your cards are pretty much aligned with your expectation, you figure to be a big winner. And the reason you have such a large positive expectation is that the size of the pot far exceeded the odds against making your hand.

Three Rules for Considering Pot Odds and Implied Odds

While there are always caveats that might cause you to deviate from these suggestions, here are three rules of thumb to think about when you're considering the pot odds/implied odds relationship.

- If you are a money favorite on new money entering the pot on the current betting round alone—

forget, for a second, about the money that's already in the pot—you should bet or raise to build the pot. If you've flopped a flush draw, are last to act, and five players have already called, go ahead and raise. You are getting a big enough price on this betting round alone to justify your action. The odds against completing your hand on the turn when flopping a four-flush are approximately 4-to-1 against you. But you're getting 5-to-1 on new money entering the pot—never mind the money already in it. So, put some more money in the pot, and do it now.

- If you are a money favorite because of the size of the pot or the implied odds you think you'll get if you make your hand, calling is usually the best option. If you ignore the fact that raising may allow you to win the pot by causing your opponents to fold, raising in these situations only reduces your implied odds. Now is the time to make your hand inexpensively—even if some wealthy lunatic just sauntered by and dropped a few five-thousand dollar chips in the pot.

- If you have neither pot odds, nor implied odds, and are not a money favorite, fold and save your money.

When Oscar Wilde wrote, "The truth is rarely pure, and never simple," he was probably not thinking about a poker game, but his words hold true nonetheless. These three rules of thumb are not the entire answer, of course. While it's easy to come up with a raft of reasons to deviate from them on occasion, the fact remains that the relationship between pot odds, implied odds, the odds against making your hand, and money that's already in the pot will go a long way toward answering that age-old poker conundrum: Shall I fold, bet, call, or raise?

Figuring Pot Odds

Figuring pot odds is a necessary part of any poker player's game. Without it, we don't have any way of knowing whether the odds against making our hand are offset by this fundamental relationship: How much will it cost to keep playing this hand, and how much money am I likely to win if I catch the card I need? By understanding the relationship between the odds against making our hand and the money we figure to win if we get lucky, we can play skillful high percentage poker instead of treating the game like some form of *gambling*.

These calculations involve comparing the total number of unknown cards with the number of cards that will complete your hand—the *outs*—then doing a bit of division. For example, whenever you hold four cards to the nut flush on the turn in a Texas Hold'em game, there are 46 unknown cards (52 minus your 2 pocket cards and 4 on the board). Of those 46 cards, 37 cards won't help you, but those other 9 cards are the same suit as your flush draw and any one of them will give you the nut flush.

The odds are 4-to-1, against making your draw. Percentage poker players will call a bet in this situation only if the pot is four times the size of the bet. In a $20–$40 game, the pot would need to contain at least $160—or else you'd have to be able to count on winning at least a total of $160 from future calls—the implied odds—to satisfy this requirement.

If you're the kind of player who's fond of inside straights and other long-shot draws, consider this: You have only four outs on the turn. That's not much when you consider that forty-two of the remaining cards won't help you at all. The chances of you completing your hand are less than 9 percent. If you'd prefer expressing that figure as odds instead of as a percentage, here's the bad news. The odds against completing your inside straight draw are 10.5-to-1, and you'd need a pot that's more than ten times the cost of your call in order to make it worthwhile.

If you had two pair and knew for a fact that your opponent had a flush, you'd be in the same predicament, since only four of the remaining cards in the deck will elevate two pair to a full house. When can you play hands like this? On two occasions: After you hit the multistate Powerball lottery and win ninety million dollars or so. Then, $20–$40 hold'em becomes the equivalent of playing for matchsticks. The other occasion is in a game with complete maniacs whose collective motto is: "All bets called, all the time." You would need to win more than ten times the amount of your call to justify this kind of draw. But if you figure to win a $450 pot by calling a $40 bet with an inside straight draw, go ahead. Go for it.

A Cheat Sheet for Figuring Odds and Outs

If you memorize the chart that follows, you won't have to waste even a fraction of a second doing arithmetic at the poker table. Personally, we find it tough concentrating on the cards in play *and* our opponents while trying to do calculations at the poker table. Fortunately, there are simplified methods that approximate the percentage of time you'll be able to make your hand.

An easy method involves multiplying your outs by two, then adding two to that sum. The result is a rough percentage of the chance you have of making your hand from the turn to the river. Suppose you have a flush draw on the turn: You have nine outs (9 x 2 = 18, and 18 + 2 = 20). That's pretty close to the 19.6 percent chance you'd come up with if you worked out the answer mathematically.

The strategic implications of this are simple: If you have a 10 percent chance of winning, the cost of your call should not be more than 10 percent of the pot's total. With a 32 percent chance, you can call a bet up to one-third the size of the pot.

While the "outs times 2 plus 2" method is an easy calculation to make at the poker table, it's even easier to commit the chart to memory. That way you never have to figure a thing. Just tap into your memory bank and pull out the correct figure. Any time you find yourself fighting a tinge of self-doubt, you can always double-check yourself using the "outs times 2 plus 2" approximation.

If you want to estimate your chances on the flop without the need for much arithmetic, try this: If you have between one and eight outs, quadruple them. Eight outs multiplied by four yields 32, while the precise answer is 31.5 percent. With four outs, the quadrupling method yields 16 percent, while the accurate answer is 16.5 percent.

With nine outs—a common situation, because it represents the number of outs to a four-flush—quadruple the number of outs and subtract one. You'll be spot-on when you do, since the arithmetical answer is 35 percent. You can use this method up to twelve outs, though with twelve outs our shortcut method yields 47 percent, while the precise answer is only 45 percent.

For thirteen through sixteen outs, quadruple the number of outs, subtract four, and your results won't be any more than 2 percent off dead center. And remember, any time you find yourself with fourteen outs or more, you are an odds-on favorite to make your hand; pot odds of any size become worthwhile.

The chart on page 211 shows odds against making your hand with two cards to come (flop to river), as well as with one card (turn to river) remaining.

Hanging on to unprofitable draws for whatever reason—and many players persist in drawing to long shots even when they really do know better—can be a major leak in one's game. For many, it's the sole reason they are lifelong losing players instead of lifelong winners.

There's no real excuse for that kind of play, even if you are not mathematically inclined (and if you're in this category, you're in the majority). Most people we know loathe doing calculations while playing poker, but now you have two sure-fire ways to get the answers. And you don't have to do anything more difficult than multiplying by two or four, or memorizing a simple chart. Just count the size of the pot, or even approximate it, compare one to the other, and make your decision. It's that easy.

Controlling the Odds and Manipulating Them to Your Advantage

One of the major differences between fixed-limit poker games and pot- or no-limit games is that in the latter two, you're able to manipulate the size of the pot, and the odds offered to your opponent, by virtue of the size of your bet. In a fixed-limit game, the amount you can wager is predetermined. You can either bet or not, but you won't be able to do much to manipulate the pot odds offered your opponent.

Here's a simple example, and to make it crystal clear, let's assume you and one opponent are contesting a pot on the turn. Both of you have your cards face up. While that's

ODDS AND OUTS ON THE FLOP AND ON THE TURN

Outs	Common Draws	Flop to the River Percent	Odds	Turn to the River Percent	Odds
20		67.5	0.48-to-1	43.5	1.30-to-1
19		65.0	0.54-to-1	41.3	1.42-to-1
18		62.4	0.60-to-1	39.1	1.56-to-1
17		59.8	0.67-to-1	37.0	1.71-to-1
16		57.0	0.75-to-1	34.8	1.88-to-1
15	Straight Flush	54.1	0.85-to-1	32.6	2.07-to-1
14		51.2	0.95-to-1	30.4	2.29-to-1
13		48.1	1.08-to-1	28.3	2.54-to-1
12		45.0	1.22-to-1	26.1	2.83-to-1
11		41.7	1.40-to-1	23.9	3.18-to-1
10		38.4	1.60-to-1	21.7	3.60-to-1
9	Flush	35.0	1.86-to-1	19.6	4.11-to-1
8	Straight	31.5	2.17-to-1	17.4	4.75-to-1
7		27.8	2.60-to-1	15.2	5.57-to-1
6		24.1	3.15-to-1	13.0	6.67-to-1
5		20.3	3.93-to-1	10.9	8.20-to-1
4	Two pair or Inside Straight Draw	16.5	5.06-to-1	8.7	10.50-to-1
3		12.5	7.00-to-1	6.5	14.33-to-1
2		8.4	10.90-to-1	4.3	22.00-to-1
1		4.3	22.26-to-1	2.2	45.00-to-1

Other Probabilities:

A wired pair flops a set nearly 12 percent of the time.

If you are dealt A-K, you'll flop at least one ace or king 32.4 percent of the time.

Two suited cards will make a flush 6.5 percent of the time.

Two suited cards flops a flush 0.8 percent of the time.

Two suited cards flops a four flush 10.9 percent of the time.

Two unmatched cards will make a split pair 2.2 percent of the time.

not likely to happen unless one of you is all-in during a tournament, by having you play this hand face up, neither of you can draw an incorrect conclusion about the hand your opponent is holding.

You have top pair with the best possible kicker. Your opponent has four cards to a flush. If he makes his flush, he wins. If he fails to make a flush, you win a $200 pot.

If the betting limit is $20 and you bet, your opponent will win $220 every time he makes his flush. He'll lose $20 when he doesn't. If we don't count your two face-up cards—remember, this is an extreme example just to make a point and things won't ever play out like this in a real game—forty-six unknown cards remain in the deck. There were fifty-two to start with, and your opponent has seen two in his hand and four on the board, leaving forty-six that aren't known to him. Of those forty-six unknown cards, nine will complete his flush (thirteen of each suit in a deck, minus the four cards of that suit that are in his hand and on the board). The odds against making a flush are 37-to-9. Call it 4-to-1. That's close enough.

What does this mean? The answer is simple. Because the pot offers your opponent a potential of $220 for a $20 wager, which is 11-to-1 on his money, and he's only a 4-to-1 underdog to make his hand, he needs to call your bet. He'll profit in the long run by doing so because the pot odds *exceed* the odds against making his hand.

You made no mistake either, because you are a 4-to-1 favorite to win the hand. If you failed to bet, you'd have given your opponent infinite odds to draw for his hand. Failing to bet would have been a much worse play than betting, even though you know your opponent is getting the correct price to call, and will profit in the long run from doing so.

If you were playing no-limit, the story line plays out differently. Now you could bet $200 into that pot—or $400, or as much as you had in front of you. If you wagered $400, the pot would contain $600, but your opponent would have to invest $400 for a chance to win it. Your large wager manipulated the price the pot is offering your opponent to 3-to-2. But the odds against completing his flush remain unchanged at 4-to-1. The pot odds are now much smaller than the chance of making his hand, and in the long run your opponent would lose a lot of money by calling.

Even if you were playing pot-limit and could only bet the size of the pot, which in this case would be $200, your opponent would be forced to call a $200 bet for a chance to win $400. While 2-to-1 is a lot better than 3-to-2, your opponent's odds of making a flush are still 4-to-1. While he'll lose less money in the long run calling this bet instead of calling a bet offering him only 3-to-2, he'll lose money in the long run nevertheless—and he'll continue to do so as long as the pot odds are not offering him at least 4-to-1 odds. If the pot odds and odds against making his hand were identical, it wouldn't make any difference in the long run whether he calls or folds; it's a break-even proposition.

While this example is simple, the skill of manipulating the pot so that your opponent gets a poor price to draw for his hand is a technique that every successful pot-limit or no-limit player has mastered. By manipulating the size of the pot, the professional player knows that he can create situations where his opponent will either err by calling his bet or surrender the pot by folding!

The choice of how much to bet, which never comes into play in a fixed-limit game is another tool at the disposal of skilled players who have learned how to use them to their advantage. And used properly it can lead to "heads

I win, tails you lose" situations most of the time that translate into accelerated winnings for players who have learned this technique.

Basic Arithmetic

Many of the choices you have to make at the poker table are based on numbers. You always find yourself in search of the answer to poker's *Prime Question:* "Are the odds against making my hand offset by the money in the pot or the money that *figures to be in the pot* by the end of the hand?" If you can answer this question correctly most of the time, you are on your way to resolving many of the dilemmas you'll encounter at the poker table.

Suppose the odds are 2-to-1 against making your hand. The pot will pay three dollars for each dollar you must invest in order to try and catch that winning card. In this case, it pays to call. In fact, if you figure to attract more than two dollars for each dollar wagered *on that particular betting round*, it even pays to bet your draw aggressively.

If the relationship between the odds against making your hand and the pot were different, and you figured to make your hand only one time in four attempts, you'd better not call if the pot only appears to be offering a 2-to-1 return on your money.

One comforting feature about hold'em is that situations frequently repeat themselves. So, even if you are *innumerate*—a word that describes those of us who are "illiterate" where numbers are concerned—you can simply memorize the odds against catching the card you need in certain situations, compare it to the pot odds, and your answer becomes obvious.

Don't worry if you have a hard time counting the pot.

You don't need to be all that precise about it and a close estimate will usually suffice. But when you do count the pot, be sure to consider how many additional bets you're likely to win from those opponents who will probably call if you make your hand.

When you play hold'em, there are many other situations where your decision about whether to continue playing once you see the flop will be based on the size of the pot compared to the odds against making your hand—but these will do for starters. If you memorize these odds, and can make a reasonable estimate about how many opponents will pay you off if you make your hand, you won't go too far afield.

Count Your Opponents

The more opponents in the pot, the more straightforward poker you should play. Suppose you hold A-K, and three small cards flop. What should you do? The answer depends, at least in part, on the number of opponents you are facing. If the flop didn't hit your hand, but there are seven other active players, you can almost be certain the flop was kind to someone. If there's a bet and a call, consider this: To win, an ace or king needs to fall on the turn or the river, and it cannot give your opponents two pair. In addition, you have to hope you are not up against two pair, or better, already.

How do you assess whether you're up against two pair? Look at the flop. If the flop were 10-9-7 or J-10-9 chances of two pair are greater than they would be with a flop like J-6-3. Why? Most players will call with connected cards, or cards with a small gap, much more often than they will with an absolutely ragged hand like J-6, J-3, or 6-3.

The Magic Number Is Two

Against only one or two opponents, your A-K may be the best hand regardless of whether the flop helps your hand. But if you are contesting the pot against more than two opponents, you need to be extremely careful. With a multitude of opponents, any flop that doesn't help you probably helps one of your opponents. When that's the case, "fit or fold" is usually the best course of action. If you need a metric to guide you, the breakage point is usually two or three. One or two opponents and you stand a chance of winning even when big cards like A-K don't improve. Against three opponents or more, your chances will decrease progressively—from slim to none—based on the number of opponents contesting the pot.

The more opponents, the less bluffing you should do. It's nearly impossible to bluff seven players and it's foolish to even try. After all, the flop that missed you probably hit one of your opponents, and he's the one who will call your bet. But if you are up against only one or two opponents, you might be able to steal the pot often enough to make a propitious bluff pay off.

Game Theory Without Games

Game theory has long been applicable to poker. Nesmith C. Ankeny first discussed it in *Poker Strategy: Winning With Game Theory*, a book published in 1981. David Sklansky also discussed game theory two years later in his seminal work, *Winning Poker*.

Despite its name, game theory is not about Monopoly, or Hearts, or fantasy football. It's a branch of mathematics that deals with decision-making and has applicability in fields as diverse as economics, political science, operations research, military science, and poker too—where the idea is to *optimize* a decision rather than to maximize or minimize any one of a multitude of possible choices.

Suppose you're heads up in a poker game after all the cards have been dealt, and you know nothing about your opponent. You've never played against him before and haven't been able to pick up even the slightest inkling of a tell. In fact, we'll just assume you're playing against the Invisible Man. You don't have much of a hand—nothing more, actually, than a busted flush—and the only way you can win is by bluffing successfully. To complete this set up, let's assume your opponent cannot beat a flush, but his hand is strong enough to beat any busted flush.

Here's where game theory comes into play. Suppose you decide to bet every flush draw whether you make it or not. What do you think would happen? A cautious opponent would throw his hand away most of the time, and you'd win the pot whenever he did. But if your adversary plays well, he'd begin to suspect you of larceny and would call with increasing regularity. Once he pegs you as a habitual bluffer, he will call every time you come out betting. Now the situation has reversed itself. Rather than winning each time you came out betting, you'd lose much of the time. Only your legitimate hands would win, but your opponent would win a pot that now includes one additional bet whenever you bluffed.

Suppose you took the opposite tack by never bluffing. Now you bet only when you make a legitimate hand. Just as he did when you bluffed too often, your opponent would quickly sort things out and once he realized that you never bluff, he would adjust his strategy accordingly by folding when you bet and showing down the best hand whenever you checked.

One Dimensional Play Will Cause You to Lose Control of the Situation as Soon as Your Opponent Figures You Out

Do you see what's happening here? Not only was your opponent able to clock your pattern of bluffing whenever you had a drawing hand that did not materialize, but your results were never a function of your own actions. Instead, the results you achieved were wholly dependent on your opponent's decision. You were not in charge. Your playing strategy allowed the locus of control to pass to your opponent, who, by virtue of his calling or folding decisions, was the one who determined how much you won or lost.

It's pretty clear from all of this that you can't be a one-dimensional player, and you don't have to know about an arcane branch of mathematics called game theory to tell you that. Even if you only bluffed once in a blue moon, or refrained from bluffing just this once—no matter how much you'd really like to steal that pot—you'd establish opportunities for your opponent to make errors by forcing him to make a decision about the legitimacy of your hand. If you always bluff, or never bluff your opponent isn't given a chance to make a mistake. If he knows you bluff all the time or realizes that you never bluff at all—either way it makes no difference—his strategy is as easy as it is obvious, and he will maximize his winnings as a result.

Varying Your Play Gives Your Opponent a Chance to Make a Mistake

But when you veer away from polar extremes, your opponent is put to the test: Do you or don't you have the goods? And you know what? Whenever you give your opponent a chance to make mistakes, some mistakes will be made. He will, we will, and every player who's ever lived makes errors in judgment. In poker, no one makes the right decision all the time; it's a game of incomplete information, and in the absence of absolute certainty, wrong decisions are made.

Game theory provides the wherewithal to optimize decision-making. It guarantees that when you bluff with a certain frequency, it will not matter how your opponent responds. Game theory allows you to control the outcome of your actions and *optimize*—while neither maximizing nor minimizing—the results you achieve.

How to Use Game Theory to Bluff Optimally

Here's how to bluff using game theory: Make sure the odds against your bluff are equal to the odds your opponent is getting from the pot. Confusing? Not really. Suppose your bet creates a situation where your opponent will be getting 4–to–1 odds from the pot. That's easy to imagine. The pot already contains $300. By calling your $100 bet, your opponent stands to win $400 if he shows down the best hand.

Now, let's say any one of eight available cards will give you the winning hand. If you bluff whenever two predetermined cards come up, in addition to the eight you need, you are bluffing at a frequency that precludes your opponent from taking advantage of your bluffing proclivities—regardless of what he chooses to do. Since eight-to-two is the same as four-to-one, you are bluffing at a rate that is optimal from a game theory perspective. Even if you told your opponent you were going to bluff using game theory as a way to determine the optimal frequency for bluffing, there's not a thing your opponent can do to nullify this. Nothing. Nada.

How to Randomize Your Bluffing Attempts

How easy is that to pull off? You can trigger your bluff versus no-bluff decision by randomizing it with cards. Suppose you are looking for either a seven or a queen to complete your hand. Any one of those eight cards will do; it doesn't matter which one pops out of the deck. Now suppose you tell yourself that you will also come out bluffing if your last card is a red deuce instead of the hoped-for seven or queen. Now you've given yourself two bluffing cards—randomly selected. That's critically important—as well as eight winning cards in the 4-to-1 ratio of winning cards to your opponent's pot odds, thus optimizing your results.

Another way to randomize your bluffs is by using your wristwatch to trigger them. In a four-to-one situation, just divide a minute into twelve second segments. Five, twelve-second segments comprise each minute. If you want a 4-to-1 situation, just use the first forty-eight seconds as a signal not to bluff, and the last twelve second segment (from forty-eight seconds to the top of your watch) as a bluffing trigger. All you have to do is glance at your watch, notice where the second hand is at the instant you first see it, and allow that to randomly determine your bluffing decisions.

But there is a rub. It's tough to make these kinds of calculations in the heat of battle. Most players don't do this sort of thing; trust us, they really don't. Nevertheless, you can work out common drawing situations in advance, just like we did here, and you don't even have to be absolutely precise. Oh, sure, it's stylish to be right on the money, mathematically speaking. As long as you realize that to play winning poker you have to allow yourself the opportunity to make mistakes at the polar extremes—neither habitually bluffing nor always checking, nor always calling your opponent's wager or folding every time he bets—to avoid making more costly mistakes in the middle.

Game Theory Is No Substitute for Knowing Your Opponents

When all is said and done, you're not even going to use game theory all that often at the table. The more you play, and the better able you are to read your opponent—putting him on a hand, as it were, and picking up tells—the less you'll have to rely on game theory. After all, you usually won't be playing against the Invisible Man. Even if you play online, where your opponents actually *are* invisible, you can discover tells and read them for hands based on their proclivities for checking versus betting and calling versus folding.

Game theory is pretty cool stuff. We all owe a debt of gratitude to Ankeny and Sklansky for presenting it so cogently. However, its greatest value probably lies in assisting us to learn how often to bluff for value, as well as how frequently to fold or try to snap off your opponent's bluff.

Learning to Do the Math Yourself

When playing hold'em, you're always dealing odds. Yet to many of us, math is off-putting, to say the least. Some of us are downright phobic about it. But poker math need not be difficult, and you won't need anything more sophisticated than basic arithmetic to follow along.

There are only 169 unique, two-card starting hands that you might be dealt when you're playing Texas hold'em. This figure of 169 assumes that A♠A♥ is identical to A♣A♦, and that A♥Q♥ is equal to A♦Q♦. Here's how to figure it.

You'll be dealt any of thirteen distinct ranks, from ace up through king, as your first or second card. All you need do, therefore, is multiply thirteen by thirteen to calculate the correct answer.

But it's not the *whole truth*. Why? Because things might be different after the flop. A three-suited flop can certainly make some holdings much more valuable than others. If the flop contained three diamonds, wouldn't you rather have the ace of diamonds in your hand than any other ace?

While there are *169 different starting hands,* there are also *1,326 different two-card combinations*. It all depends when you look at your hand. Before the flop there's no real point in distinguishing between hands like A♥Q♥ and A♠Q♠ because you have no idea what suits will jump out of the deck on the flop. But after the flop, those suits might matter enough to make you fold one hand but raise with another, even though they were equivalent before the flop.

It also makes a difference when you're figuring the odds against certain combinations of starting hands. Then you'll want to deal with all of the 1,326 different two-card combinations.

Here's an example. Suppose the woman sitting next to you would raise only with aces, kings, or A-K, and you're holding a pair of queens. Do you think you're ahead or behind in the hand right now?

It's not difficult to figure this. The only hands better than a pair of queens at this point are a pair of aces or a pair of kings. Queens, after all, are stronger than A-K right now, since A-K has to improve on or after the flop in order to beat you.

How to Figure the Number of Ways to Make a Pair

So before we go any further, we have to know the number of different ways we can make a pair of aces or a pair of kings, as well as the number of ways we can make A-K, and then compare the two.

Here is each and every way for you to make a pair of aces, or any pair, for that matter. A♠A♦, A♠A♣, A♠A♥, A♦A♣, A♦A♥, and A♥A♣. You'll be able to figure this out just by taking the aces out of a deck and moving them around until you've combined them in every way possible. If you do this, you'll come up with the correct answer even if you don't know how to do the math.

But the math is simple. What you've done just by laying out all the possible ways you might make a pair of aces is called a *combination*. By arranging the aces so that you could track each and every possible way you could make a pair of aces from the four that are in the deck, you provided the answer to this question: "How many ways can you *choose* two items (in this case, each possible pair of aces) from a *universe* of four aces?"

From a mathematical perspective, what you did involved multiplying components of the *universe* in descending, but sequential order. And you did this instinctively, even if you were unaware of the arithmetic involved. You did this by selecting as many components as there were *choices*. That was step one. Then you multiplied each component of your *choices* in ascending order. That's step two. That sounds a lot more complex than it really is.

In our example with the aces, you multiplied 4 x 3, or 12, and then you multiplied 2 x 1, or 2. The next step is to set up a division problem. The product of the *universe* calculation is on top (the number on top is called the *numerator*) and the product of the *choice* calculation is on the bottom (the *denominator*). Then divide the numerator by the denominator. The answer, of course, is 12/2, or six.

To figure out how many ways you can *choose* four items out of a universe of twenty items, you'd multiply (20 x 19 x

18 x 17 = 116,280). Now, divide by the following product (4 x 3 x 2 x 1). The answer works out to be 4,845. You can *cancel out* numbers to simplify the calculation. Just as long as you treat both the numerator and denominator the same, you can't go wrong. In this problem, you can divide the 4 in the denominator by 4, yielding 1, and 20 in the numerator by 4, which yields 5. You can also divide 3 by 3 to yield 1, and 18 by 3, which yields 6. Then you can divide 2 by itself, and 6 by 2. This simplifies the problem to: (5 x 19 x 3 x 17 ÷ 1). Canceling out can simplify problems. When you are working with large numbers, it will keep your pocket calculator from giving you an error message.

How Many Ways Can I Make Big Slick or Any Other Two-Card Combination?

It's even easier determining how many ways you can make A-K. There are four aces and four kings—and since any of the aces can combine with any of the kings, the answer is sixteen. It's a simple case of multiplying four times four. The reason you can't simply multiply when calculating how many pairs of aces can be extracted from a four-ace universe is because aces can't combine with themselves. But each ace can combine with each king. So, there are sixteen ways to make Big Slick.

With six ways to make a pair of aces, six ways to make a pair of kings, but sixteen ways to make A-K, chances are greater that he raised with A-K because sixteen ways to make A-K exceeds the twelve ways to make either a pair of aces or a pair of kings!

What Are the Odds Against Being Dealt a Pocket Pair of Aces?

Another useful calculation you can do with what you've learned thus far is to determine the odds against being dealt a pair of aces (or any other specific pair) before the flop. Since there are six ways to make a pair of aces, all you have to do is divide 1,326 by 6 to figure this out. That's easy. You'll receive aces, on average, once every 221 hands. Expressed in odds, you are a 220-to-1 underdog. That's why people get so upset when they are finally dealt a pair of aces and lose with them. Pocket aces don't come around all that often. Losing with them is like finding out that your birthday has been taken away.

You can also figure out the percentage of starting hands you raise with. If you were to raise with any pair of 10s or higher, as well as A-K, A-Q, A-J, K-Q, or K-J, you've chosen five pairs (T-T, J-J, Q-Q, K-K, A-A, each of which can be made six ways) or thirty paired hands you'll raise with, as well as five combinations of big cards (which can each be made in 16 ways) or 80 big cards. The total (80 + 30) equals 110 raising hands. Since there are 1,326 possibilities, you'll probably raise about 8 percent of the time (110/1326) x 100 = 8.3 percent.

How Many Possible Flops Are There?

To figure out how many possible flops there are, you'll have to determine the number of three-card combinations that can be selected from a *universe* of fifty cards. Why fifty, and not fifty-two? We're interested in the universe of *unknown* cards, and the two cards in your hand are excluded because you know what they are. You also know that they cannot appear both in your hand and on the flop. Your opponents also have two cards each, but because you don't know what they are, you have to assume that *any* of the fifty unknown cards are equally likely to appear on the flop. If you happened to get a peek at one of your opponents' cards, then the universe would be reduced to forty-nine—since you would also know with complete certainty that any exposed cards won't make it to the flop either.

Figuring this out is just like the calculations we did in determining how many ways you could make a pair of aces from a universe of four aces. However, only this calculation requires dividing the product of (50 x 49 x 48) by (1 x 2 x 3). If you don't *cancel out* to simplify the calculations, just divide 117,600 by 6 and you'll learn that there are 19,600 possible flops, no more and no less. That's a handy number to know because you can use it to determine your chances of flopping a set, or better, anytime you start out with a pair in your hand.

If I Start with a Pair, How Often Will I Flop a Set?

It's easy. If you figure the number of ways to flop a set when you start with a pair in the hole, you can compare that number with the 19,600 combinations that comprise the universe of possible flops.

Take our word for it; the easiest way to do this is to determine the number of ways to *miss* making a set. Suppose you were dealt J♦J♣. Of the fifty unknown cards remaining in the deck, two other jacks will form *at least* a set. We're going to exclude the remote possibility that the flop itself is a set. If the flop was 8♣8♠8♥, any opponent holding a bigger pocket pair now has a bigger full house, and if someone holds the 8♦, he's made quads, an almost unbeatable hand.

Forget about those monsters under the bed. If the two remaining jacks are the only two cards that will form a set, the other forty-eight cards won't get you there. If the first card up on the flop is not a jack, then forty-seven of the remaining forty-nine cards also misfired, and if the second card brings no help, that third and final flop card will not be a jack 46 out of 48 times.

Your next step is simple. Just multiply the fractions as follows (48/50 x 47/49 x 46/48). Multiplying the numerators (top numbers, or 48 x 47 x 46) you get 103,776. When the denominators are multiplied the answer is 117,600.

This means you *won't* flop a set or better 103,776 out of 117,600 times. And if you subtract the 103,776 misses from the universe of 117,600, you are left with 13,824 hits. You'll flop a set or better 13,824 out of 117,600 times.

But fractions that large are unwieldy. To reduce it, divide the numerator and denominator by 13,824. When you do, you'll find yourself left with 1/8.5. If a percentage is more to your liking, just divide 1 by 8.5 (or 13,824 by 117,600). You'll wind up with 0.118. If you multiply that by 100, you'll have converted that fraction to a percentage, and you'll flop a set or better 11.8 percent of the time that you hold a pair in your hand.

Changing Odds to Percentages and Back Again

Poker players are often more comfortable talking about odds than percentages. Here's how to go about converting odds to percentages and vice-versa. But, first, it's important to clarify what is meant by *odds*. Odds are a *ratio of failures to successes*, where the first number represents the predicted *failures*, and the second number is the expectation of *successful events*.

Here's what you're saying when you ask, "What are the odds?" You really mean, "What are the odds *against* an event occurring," or, "What is the predicted ratio of failures to successes?" If the odds against your horse winning are 8-to-5, it means that if this race were to be run thirteen times (8 + 5), your horse figures to win five of those races and lose eight of them.

Understanding the relationship between percentages and odds will help whether you're betting on horses, playing cards, or just contemplating the chances that it's going to rain. To change a percentage to odds, subtract the percentage from 100; then divide the result by that same percentage. If something has a 40 percent chance of occurring, this is the calculation: (100 − 40) ÷ 40, or 60/40, which equates to 1.5. Thus the *odds against* something that has a 40 percent chance of occurring are 1.5-to-1.

Reversing your field and converting odds to a percentage is just as easy. If the odds against your horse winning are 8-to-5, you figure to win your bet five times out of thirteen tries. You came up with 13 because odds are a *ratio* of failures to successes. If you add the failures to the successes, you have a *universe* of 13 events. If you estimate your horse will win 5 times out of 13 trials, just divide the expected wins by the universe of events, or divide 5 by 13. You've also figured that if the odds against your horse winning are 8-to-5, the chance of him winning is 38 percent.

Try it yourself, assuming odds of 7-to-2. Add 7 and 2 and you get 9. If you divide 2 by 9, the result is 22 percent. Now you know that a 7-to-2 shot has a 22 percent chance of winning. If you've been able to follow this so far, take the time to work out some additional problems.

Figuring the Odds for Straights and Flushes

Flopping a four-flush or a four to a straight happens regularly when you play hold'em. Knowing the odds against making either of these hands, when compared with the pot odds, provides the information you'll need to decide if your drawing hands have a positive expectation in the long run.

Calculating pot odds is easy. Just count the size of the pot and compare it to the cost of calling a bet. You can also estimate how much money figures to be in the pot at the end of the hand. Compare that against your *expected* investment. When money odds exceed drawing odds, you have the best of it. Otherwise, you're *drawing long*.

Because straight and flush draws are so common in hold'em, we'll take a special look at these relationships. Suppose you have K♥9♥ and the flop is 6♥7♣2♥. With thirteen cards of each suit in a deck, you've accounted for four of them and only nine of the remaining forty-seven cards can be hearts.

Once again, it's easier to calculate the number of ways to *miss* your flush, by subtracting the misses from the universe of possibilities. The result is the answer.

There are forty-seven unknown cards once you've seen the flop. Since nine are hearts, the remaining thirty-eight will not help you. If you miss your flush on the turn, there are only forty-six unknown cards. Nine of them are hearts, and the remaining thirty-seven won't help you. Once again, we're going to multiply fractions. Multiply the numerator of the first fraction by the numerator of the second. Then perform the same calculation for the denominators. The result: $38/47 \times 37/46 = 1,406/2,162$.

If you subtract 1,406, which represents the number of times you won't make your flush, from the 2,162 possible events, you are left with 756 combinations that result in a flush. Now divide 756 by 2,162. The answer is 0.35 (or 35 percent). If you flop a four-flush, you'll make your flush 35 percent of the time.

To convert that percentage into odds, just subtract 35 percent from 100 percent. Then divide that by 35 percent (100 − 35 = 65; 65 ÷ 35 = 1.86) and you've determined that the odds against completing your flush are 1.86-to-1. If the pot figures to pay 2-to-1 or more on your investment, drawing to make your flush will be profitable in the long run, regardless of what happens on this particular hand.

Every professional poker player, and every skilled amateur who wins steadily at the game, takes the best of it most of the time. What separates winning players from the rest of the pack is this simple fact: *Winning players take the gamble out of poker*.

Figuring the odds against making a straight is very similar to the flush problem. In fact, the process is identical; only the numbers change.

If you hold 9♦8♦, and the flop is K♣7♠6♥, you've flopped an *open-ended* straight draw. Either a ten or a five completes your straight. Since there are four of each in the deck, any of those eight cards will complete your hand.

It's time to multiply fractions. You'll *miss* your straight 39 times out of 47 on the turn, and 38 times out of 46 on the river. Multiply 39/47 x 38/46, and you'll figure out that you won't make a straight 1,482 times out of 2,162 attempts. Just subtract the misses from the universe of possibilities (2,162 − 1,482). You'll have determined that a straight will be made 680 times for every 2,162 times you flop an open-ended straight draw.

Divide 680 by 2,162 to learn that you'll complete a straight 31.5 percent of the time. Do the conversion and that equates to odds of 2.17-to-1 against making your hand. It's not that far off from the odds against making a flush. But a four-flush will be completed more frequently than four-to-a-straight will be completed. And that stands to reason because there are nine cards to complete a flush but only eight to complete a straight.

How Often Will I Flop at Least a Pair with Ace-King?

Do you usually raise with A-K or do you prefer to call and see if you get lucky on the flop? Before you decide, we'll show you how often you'll flop at least a pair with this holding. After all, while Big Slick is a huge drawing hand, it usually must improve to provide much more than bluffing value.

Because you already hold one ace and one king in your hand, there are only three more aces and three more kings among the remaining fifty unknown cards in the deck, along with forty-four cards that won't help you. Forty-four out of fifty times, you won't catch an ace or a king on the flop's first card. If the first card misses, there are still six good cards left in the deck, along with forty-three of the remaining forty-nine that won't help you. If neither the first and second card are an ace or a king, six good cards and forty-two bad ones comprise the forty-eight unknown cards left in the deck. Multiply 44/50 x 43/49 x 42/48, and you'll come up with 79,464/117,600. When you subtract those 79,464 ways you can miss catching at least an ace or a king from the universe of 117,600 possible combinations, you're left with 38,136 ways to improve to at least a pair of aces or kings.

Dividing 117,600 into 38,136 shows that 32.4 percent of the time you'll catch at least an ace or king—which equates to odds of 2.1-to-1 against improving A-K on the flop. While that doesn't provide a definitive answer to the question of whether raising or calling is a better strategy, at least you have a few *facts* on hand when you ponder this problem.

Here's a handy chart showing the chances of making your hand based on the number of outs you have on the flop, along with the odds against making it, for situations ranging from 15 outs, where you are an *odds-on* favorite, to one out, where you're a decided long shot.

Outs	Chance of Success (%)	Odds Against Success
15	54.1	0.8-to-1
14	51.2	1.0-to-1
13	48.1	1.1-to-1
12	45.0	1.2-to-1
11	41.7	1.4-to-1
10	38.4	1.6-to-1
9	35.0	1.9-to-1
8	31.5	2.2-to-1
7	27.8	2.6-to-1
6	24.1	3.1-to-1
5	20.3	3.9-to-1
4	16.5	5.1-to-1
3	12.5	7.0-to-1
2	8.4	10.9-to-1
1	4.3	22.3-to-1

There's a lot of data in this chart, but there's no need to memorize all of it. You should memorize the percentages and odds for nine outs (flush draw); eight outs (open-ended straight draw); and four outs (two-pair draw). Even if you can't compute the others in the heat of battle, you can *interpolate*. Each additional out adds between 3 and 4 percentage points to your chances. If you have twelve outs and know that a nine-out hand has a 35 percent chance of improving, you won't be too far afield if you assume your chances of winning are between 43 and 47 percent.

Using Math to Disguise Your Hand

You can turn an opponent's draw into a play with a long-term negative expected value if you decide to bet him off of his draw. In no-limit or pot limit, you can also bet a smaller amount to encourage him to call your bet. It all depends on just how strong a hand you have.

So, how do you decide whether to occasionally play your big hands as though they were smaller and somewhat weaker or sometimes play your smaller hands as though they were bigger? While you can't reduce poker down to a formula, here are some guidelines to help with this decision:

- If you're holding a really huge hand—suppose you flopped a full house—you usually won't mind giving your opponents a chance to improve. The way to do this is to bet or raise a token amount, hope they improve enough to think they have the best hand, and take as many of their chips as you can on subsequent betting rounds.
- Two suited cards on board and your opponent appears to be on the come? If the answer is yes, you need to bet enough to take away his odds. Since the odds against completing a flush draw from the flop to the river are 1.86-to-1, you have to bet enough money to make the payoff from the pot as close to 1-to-1 as you can. If your opponent only has to call a dollar to win three or four dollars, he has a bet with a long term positive expectation;

but if he has to call a dollar to win a buck-and-a-quarter, then you have the best of it and in the long run he'd be better off folding his hand.

These kinds of considerations are easy. Once you've seen the flop, five-sevenths, or 71 percent, of each player's hand is revealed. You can usually price the opposition in or out of their draws in a no-limit game. You can often do it in a pot-limit game, too.

9

GROWING AS A PLAYER

♦ ♠

When new players start winning a few sessions in a row, they begin to overestimate their own playing ability. Many of them think, after they've read the basic books, that with their newfound knowledge of tells and good starting hands, they are now expert players. They look at players who take down pots with 6♣8♣ as horrible players. They don't realize how important it is to learn how to pull off a great bluff, especially when the cards are running bad. They even start ranting at the table things like, "You called my raise with a K♥4♥?" Such players will never experience the elation of making a call on the turn with nothing but a pretend flush draw. Learning how to bluff with impunity is imperative!

Change One Thing

Figure out what's not working and change that one thing. For example, stop playing "any ace." Stop playing "any suited cards especially if one is a high card and one is a low card." Stop raising on the come when the odds don't warrant it. Stop raising to get a free card and then not taking the card for free. Stop calling when a particular player raises because you've just *personalized* the confrontation. Stop calling check-raises. Stop playing too many hands. Stop protecting your blind with trash hands. Whatever it is that is causing you to lose or lose more, stop it! And then see if your results improve. If they don't, chances are you changed the wrong thing. Try changing something else.

Face Up

When you realize that you are playing badly, it is far better to acknowledge it than to deny it. Realizing your errors shows growth and invites change, which will ultimately make you a better player. Even worse than denying your shortcomings is to bemoan them and feel sorry for yourself. And still worse than that is to castigate and punish yourself. As trite as this may sound, most poker players would benefit from carrying a sign that reads, "Learn from your mistakes."

Sometimes Losing Is Better Than Winning

Say what? Did someone not catch this typo here? This is not a typo. Repeat. This is not a typo. This is something to consider as both a micro and macrocosm of poker and life. If you've been playing too much poker, losing money in a streak so long and bleak that you can't believe it, disregarding your responsibilities and friends and family and worrying about your finances, not getting enough exercise and getting fatter and fatter, perhaps that losing streak is a blessing!!! Take a break! Go to the gym. Finish that project. Improve your business. Work more hours. Take a vacation. De-clutter your home. Poker isn't going anywhere. Perhaps the rest will help you regroup, and when you do return to

the game refreshed, rested, and with perspective, you'll figure out a way to start that winning streak. Or take Lou's advice to heart: When your poker game is off kilter, it's always
cheaper to go to the movies!

Have a Goal

Aim to put not one bad cent into a pot. Try to take home
every penny that you're entitled to. If you spend $200
chasing and making bad calls against tight players, that's
$200 you could have taken home. Even if you won $2,000,
you could have won $2,200. Why not? You know how to
play. Stop making mistakes.

One Thing You Can Do Right Now to Raise the Level of Your Game

Sometimes the truth is so self-evident, so obvious, and so
clear that all we need to do is hold fast with all our might.
Every poker player should know this, even raw beginners.
But frequently disconnects are found between information
and *know-how*, which *Webster's Collegiate Dictionary* defines as
"knowledge of how to do something smoothly and effi-
ciently."

If you can truthfully answer "yes" to the following
question there's no need for you to read any further. But if
your answer to the following question is less than an un-
equivocal "yes," keep reading.

Do You Play Your Best Game All the Time?

If you don't play your best game all the time, ask yourself
why. If you were somehow able to measure the difference
between your best game and some lesser level you play at

from time to time, you could calculate the money you are giving away by playing below your ability.

If you want to raise your game, you have to play your best game, and not slip from that lofty pedestal you're perched on when you're playing well. This ought to be easy. No new skills are needed. You don't have to learn any new ploys to spring on your unsuspecting opponents and you needn't train your mind to perform a single dreaded statistical calculation in the midst of a poker hand. All you have to do to upgrade your game is to play as well as you can. And why wouldn't you want to? Aside from whatever social gratification poker provides, if you're playing to win money, shouldn't you want to play your best?

Why Playing Your Best Game All the Time Is So Vitally Important

Professional poker players can expect to win one big bet per hour in a mid-limit game. But suppose you always played your best—never faltering—while your opponents played the way they do right now: some play well, some never play as well as they can. A few otherwise skillful players even believe in hunches and will cold-call a raise with 9-7 suited because . . . well, they just had a *hunch*. Never mind that most of the time the flop is not going to hit their 9-7 at least twice—as it probably needs to—and when they gaze up at a board that just kicked them to the curb, they'll eventually realize they cold-called a raise with *nine-high*. Ugh!

The Thinnest of Edges Can Separate Winners from Losing Players

Now if you're playing for very high limits that one big bet per hour guideline goes right out the window. Let's assume you're playing $2,000–$4,000 Texas hold'em against a group of opponents who know everything you do about poker and possibly more. But if you never play less than your best, while they slip every so often, say once a week, you might be able to beat that game for one big bet a week, or maybe even two. If you could maintain that razor thin edge, you'd win somewhere between $200,000 and $400,000 annually. One of the interesting things about poker is how razor-thin edges can turn into large sums of money at the end of the day.

In a game like that you aren't allowed the latitude to play a hunch hand. If you do, you're toast. You can get away with it in low and mid-limit games. Many of your opponents are also playing less than perfectly and their mistakes frequently offset whatever suboptimal plays you make in your own game. In essence, they're giving back the money you gave to them.

Players who stick with their best game have an almost invisible edge. It's one you'll never even see, no matter how closely you watch the game. You won't be able to assess that Joe plays perfectly all week while Tony made one error early Tuesday morning and that's the reason Joe makes $400K a year while Tony is frantically dog-paddling to keep his head above water. One bet a week won't make or break you in a mid- or lower-limit game. The edge there is not that close and most of your opponents play below their skill level a good portion of the time, too. But that's the very reason you can significantly increase the amount of money you're earning without adding any additional arrows to your quiver. Just play well all the time, and never, but never, go off-line.

The choice is yours, and it's ours, too. And when it's completely our choice—when we have no one to blame but ourselves, when we can't deflect the results we achieve because at the end of the day we either played up to our potential or we didn't—there's nowhere to run and hide when we scurry through the dark and secret caverns of our minds and think about what we achieved or why we failed.

But we never have to go into that dark side. Never. All it requires to keep the light shining is to use our desire and force of will to turn knowledge into know-how and apply it, and that's not too much to ask, is it?

Backing Up—Analyze Your Game by Reverse Engineering Your Play

Reverse engineering is a term used to cover a host of analytical processes. It most commonly crops up in situations like this: The ABC company launches a new product. Their competitor, United Widgets Incorporated, is quite likely to be the very first customer in line to buy it. They buy one, or two, or even a few dozen. They take them back to their lab and test facilities where the United Widgets Engineering Team quickly tears them down in an attempt to see whatever new features and technology ABC included in their new, improved, competing product. You can do the same thing when you play poker.

Sometimes big revelations will come from small insights and occur so quickly you don't even notice them until they spring, fully bloomed, like an oak tree from an acorn. "I'm losing on the river most of the time I call. Most of the time I call a bet on the river, I lose," is a common refrain you're likely to hear at the poker table. It's usually followed by something like this: "I know I'm stubborn, but I just don't like to let go of a hand when I go that far with it. Besides, if my opponent bets and he's bluffing, I've lost the entire pot if I fold. It only costs me one additional bet to call his hand."

That might be a revelation to our hero, but nothing new

to your ears at all. You may have heard it a thousand times before. But even if that's a new refrain, you can reverse engineer statements like these in order to analyze them.

It's true that if you *must* make an error on the river, calling is the error of choice. The price of a call is only one additional bet while the cost of releasing the winning hand in the face of a river wager can be ten bets or more, depending on the size of the pot.

Because of the potential cost, it's a huge error instead of a small, incremental one. Nevertheless, that doesn't mean that a bet on the river should always be called. There are some occasions when it pays to toss your hand away in the face of an opponent's wager.

You Should Win When You Call a Bet on the River

But that's not what this discussion is all about, is it? There's much more under the surface than deciding when to call a bet on the river and when to let go of your hand. When it's all sorted out, you should win most of the time you decide to call a bet on the river. In fact, there really should be very few occasions over the course of a session when you call on the river and lose.

After all, most of us aren't going to the river with equal hands. The circumstances where we find ourselves confronting a bet on the river can be very different. Our hero, who seems to be the caller more often than not—and losing much of the time he calls on the river—must not only be making a mistake on the river, he probably made a mistake on the turn, too. When you reverse engineer his hand, you'll find yourself not only looking at his play on the river. You'll also evaluate his decisions made on the turn, the flop, and even on his choice of starting cards. They're all contributing factors to his arrival at the river with a weak hand. Because of the size of the pot, he finds himself trapped into calling and losing a lot more often than he really should.

In a typical four-plus hour limit hold'em session, calling twice on the river with hands that lose seems typical. The rest of the time should find you either betting on the river and winning without a call, winning when you're called by an opponent, or else finding out there's no bet on the river and the hands are checked and shown down. You'll also throw your hand away when you're on a flush or straight draw that doesn't materialize and can't even beat a decent bluff.

The river plays itself much of the time. At least it should. Either you've made two pair or a set or better, completed a flush or straight draw, think your top pair with a big kicker is good enough to win—if you bet and are called—or you have a hand that's a candidate for checking down at the end. While there are some occasions when you're heads up with A-K and try to bluff an opponent who calls with something like second or third pair, those are the exceptions, not the rule.

River Decisions Are Easier Than Most

Decisions on the river are not all that tough much of the time. Your hand has either realized its potential or it's failed to do so. In any event, your hand is now bereft of potential and you can neither bet nor call because you *hope* your hand will improve on some future betting round.

At this point you've either made the hand you were hoping to make or you didn't—and if you made it, you ought to bet. After all, if you complete a hand you were building and you're unwilling to bet, why were you trying to make that hand in the first place? There's no payoff for sticking around in hopes of building second or third best hands. You want to draw to hands that will win the pot, not lose it.

The river isn't the key to any of this. Whenever a mistake is made on the river, there's a good chance that it's merely compounding a mistake made on an earlier betting round. Remember our hero, the guy who calls and loses with regularity on the river? The river's not his problem at all. If he reverse engineers his play, he should be able to sort out all the wherefores and the whys.

If you're making mistakes on earlier betting rounds, you're likely to find yourself facing a bet on the river that you decide to call. You're doing this in order to avoid the catastrophic dilemma of calling with a hand you almost certainly know will be the lesser of the two, or you toss your hand away and never really know if you folded the best hand. But the river is not the problem. It only *seems to be* because the river is where the results are revealed. There's nowhere to go from there but the next hand. The truth of the matter is that the river may be only the last visible symptom of an issue that developed far earlier.

Look at the hands you're losing with and reverse engineer your play with an eye to deciding where you should have gotten off the train. Maybe you should have exited at the turn, or quite possibly a whole lot earlier than that.

Building Second or Third Best Hands Can Be Ruinous to Your Bankroll

In poker, the best starting hand becomes the winning hand more often than not. Calling with hands that typically grow into second or third pair, such as 7-6, can get you into trouble. One of the biggest problems that occurs with smallish connectors is that when the flop hits you once, it's usually not enough of a hand to win with. If you have 8-7 and the flop is K-Q-8, you've flopped third pair, but you'll probably lose the pot unless you are fortunate enough to either catch another eight or pair your kicker on the turn or river. Building second or third pair with low percentage hands like small gapped connectors can frequently put you on the road to ruin.

When you do win with them, no one usually suspects you of having such beauties in your hand. In limit hold'em, they don't win often enough to provide a long-term positive expected value. If you begin with A-K, any pair you make will be the highest pair and you'll have the best side card too. If you begin with A-Q or A-J, you figure to make the highest ranking pair, although there is no guarantee of it. But if you begin with 7-6, you'll probably make the second or third pair on the board. That's generally a prescription for losing money.

Save those hands, if you must, for no-limit games, where you can see the flop for one bet with lots of opponents in the pot before you, and you're getting nearly infinite implied odds. If you do that and can manage your impulses and release these hands whenever they don't flop an absolutely miraculous hand for you—which will be the vast majority of the time—then you can play them.

But if you're losing too frequently at the river, just try backing up. You'll probably find that your real error occurred a lot earlier in the hand.

Growing as a Tournament Player

If you've played several tournaments and have lost, don't just stew and simmer over someone's bad call or lucky draw. Think! What were the two cards that you went out of the tournament with? Did you make a bad call? Did you aggress too much? Did you bluff too much? Did you play too tightly and allow yourself to get short-stacked too soon? Did you get desperate when you could have waited longer? Did you lose your patience? What happened? What can you do differently to make sure that next time you will do better. Of course, strive to win, but recognize your accomplishment every single time you do better than the last. And if you don't, be satisfied that you are continuously striving to improve.

10

A JOURNEY TO THE DARK SIDE

Sadly, there's a dark side to poker, too, beyond the obvious dangers inherent in a potentially addictive activity. Many pros won't share it with anyone, but we will. Before we unveil these demons for you, though, we want to stress that most players do treat the game with the respect it deserves. Very, very few players cheat or come near to cheating by looking for every angle regardless of whether it's outside the boundaries of good sportsmanship or not.

Things used to be worse, but with the professionalization and growth of the casino industry as a whole, and the advent of a newer, younger, more educated player base, poker has experienced a greening in recent years. It has done this in much the same way as billiards and bowling did a few generations ago. That said, as more honest people become aware of the shenanigans that go on, the harder it will be for the cheaters to succeed.

Collusion in Poker Tournaments

A few—and it's a very small number—of tournament pros have developed reputations for colluding. Usually this takes the form of what's called *chip dumping*, by having one member of a ring purposely lose his chips to the ring leader.

Most of the time the leader pays all or part of the entry fees for his crew and takes a big portion of his underlings' winnings. There's nothing inherently wrong with one player staking another, but it can lead to chip dumping whenever the stakor and stakee play in the same event. Even if there's no overt collusion, it creates the illusion of financial irregularities, and that can be just as bad.

Even worse is the kind of chip dumping that occurs when one player snags a few chips from his stack and actually hands them over to another, generally in the restroom during a break. This sort of thing is cheating, pure and simple, and has no place in tournament poker. It doesn't happen all that often, but when you see it, it's the sort of thing that should be reported to the tournament director immediately.

More often the way chip dumping works is that two colluders will make sure that the player with the most chips stands the best chances of winning money in the tournament. And so that player will make a big pre-flop raise that the other will call. The two work hard to go heads up. On the flop and the turn, the owner of the bigger stack will make large bets again (but not so large as to put the caller all-in). The colluder will dutifully call those bets. Then the bettor will make another bet on the river, regardless of what the card is, and the smaller stack will fold. This form of colluding is very hard to prove because the smaller stack still has chips left over and may be someone who simply has missed filling his hand.

Another form of collusion is when two players act as a team. They will trap an unsuspecting player between them, with one betting and the other raising. They want to catch the mark in the middle. The guy doing all the raising will always fold his hand before the showdown, to avoid any possible detection as a colluder. This is probably the most common kind of collusion, and it works in tournaments and cash games, online and in traditional casinos. However, it is more easily detected online because online sites retain hand histories and employ software that detects *funny* play. When that happens, an online manager can review the playing history between the two players who appear to be colluding. He can check the hand histories to see what kind of hands the team members were raising and then folding with, and when necessary, shut down the accounts of the colluders.

The Ethics of Deal Making

Is it ethical to propose and accept a deal with an opponent when you're in the money at the final table of a tournament? No one would be interested in tennis if Andy Roddick and Roger Federer were playing in the finals of Wimbledon and decided beforehand to split first and second place money right down the middle. But that happens all the time in poker tournaments. Poker players feel this is okay because it is the players who contribute their own money to the prize pool. Since it's their money that they are proposing to chop up, they see nothing wrong with this. We're hoping this will be a moot issue in the future, and it will be, as sponsors begin contributing the major share of the prize pool. With all of the interest generated by poker on television, the game is likely to attract corporate sponsorship in the near future.

When that happens, you're likely to see some rules applied to the game that have never before been applied. In addition to a dress code for players, you'll undoubtedly see rules prohibiting players from divvying up money in a tournament. Allowing this would simply dilute viewer interest in tournament poker. The sponsors will call the tune, just as they do in golf and rodeo. It's no accident that PGA golfers have to wear slacks on tour; they're not allowed to compete in shorts. Rodeo cowboys must ride in western shirts and cowboy hats. They can't ride bulls or rope steers in golf shirts and ball caps. The Rodeo Cowboys Association says so, but it's sponsorship that drives these rules.

It's not deal making, but you'll often find pot-limit players offering to run the river card twice, especially in Omaha high-only games when one player is all-in. For the best hand, running the river twice mitigates against getting a bad beat and losing a huge pot on the river. For the hand that's running behind, it's two chances to salvage something from the pot. It's not deal making exactly, rather it's a form of insurance. The player with the worst of it will propose it to his opponent as a condition for calling a big bet that would put him all-in.

Side Kitties

There's a little scam that occurs in so-called "friendly games" and informal poker clubs. If a crafty pro thinks you play too many hands and win a good number of them, he'll propose what sounds like a win-win deal. And it is— for him only. He'll suggest that you create with him a stack that will be a shared kitty between you. He'll explain that every time he wins a pot he'll put one small bet into that kitty. You'll do the same every time you win a pot. If you're new to the game and you see that he has a large stack because he's such a good player, you'll think, "Wow, that sounds like a good deal." He's hoping you'll never notice that you'll be putting much more into that kitty than him because you'll be involved in more hands. He'll probably be distracting you with friendly banter and card flashing. You'll win many small pots; he'll win the occasional big pot. He'll be folding over and over and you'll be winning hands and stoking the kitty. He can sit there, play almost no hands, and make a nice hourly sum just by sharing that kitty with you.

Is Online Poker Rigged?

You can log onto the Internet newsgroup rec.gambling. poker almost any day of the week and read posts claiming that online poker is rigged. You'll also see an equal number of posts stating that it is on the up-and-up. Most online players believe that it does not pay for online sites—most of which make oodles of money—to gamble their reputation and continued existence on dishonest practices. We believe that, too.

Most large online sites have their random number generator function audited by major accounting firms and mathematical consulting firms. Any of them would be crazy to maximize their short-term gain when they are making plenty of money on the up and up. The information that follows has been excerpted from Poker Stars Web site. They, and all of the other large online poker sites with a strong vested interest in retaining their customer base, go to great lengths to ensure that their shuffle is random, and impervious to hacking.

We understand that a use of a fair and unpredictable shuffle algorithm is critical to our software.* To ensure

*Reprinted with permission of Poker Stars.

this and avoid major problems we use two independent sources of truly random data:

- User input, including summary of mouse movements and events timing, collected from client software.
- True hardware random number generator developed by Intel . . . which uses thermal noise as an entropy source. Each of these sources itself generates enough entropy to ensure a fair and unpredictable shuffle.

Shuffle Highlights:
A deck of 52 cards can be shuffled in 52! ways. 52! is about 2^{225}. We use 249 random bits from both entropy sources (user input and thermal noise) to achieve an even and unpredictable statistical distribution.

Furthermore, we apply conservative rules to enforce the required degree of randomness; for instance, if user input does not generate the required amount of entropy, we do not start the next hand until we obtain the required amount of entropy from Intel RNG.

We use the SHA-1 cryptographic hash algorithm to mix the entropy gathered from both sources to provide an extra level of security

We also maintain a SHA-1-based pseudo-random generator to provide even more security and protection from user data attacks

To convert random bit stream to random numbers within a required range without bias, we use a simple and reliable algorithm. For example, if we need a random number in the range 0–25: we take 5 random bits and convert them to a random number 0–31; if this number is greater than 25 we just discard all 5 bits and repeat the process

This method is not affected by biases related to modulus operation for generation of random numbers that are not 2^n, $n = 1,2,...$

To perform an actual shuffle, we use another simple and reliable algorithm:

First we draw a random card from the original deck (1 of 52) and place it in a new deck—now the original deck contains 51 cards and the new deck contains 1 card.

Then we draw another random card from the original deck (1 of 51) and place it on top of the new deck—now the original deck contains 50 cards and the new deck contains 2 cards.

We repeat the process until all cards have moved from the original deck to the new deck.

11

A PLAN FOR WINNING POKER

Reading one book is never sufficient to make one a lifelong winner at poker. As with every other endeavor, learning is a lifelong issue, and serious players need to give some thought to a *plan* to continue to improve their poker.

Japanese management theorists use the term *kai zen* when they speak of "continuous improvement." It's not just a case of practicing here and there, but a conscious effort to ensure that you are improving at a more rapid rate than your opponents. It is this comparison of states of change that's of paramount importance to these management theorists, and the concept is quite relevant to poker. Poker can be taught and it can be learned, and for the player who is willing to risk some of his or her hard earned money at the tables, it's nice to know that while you might not know it all at this juncture, at least you have a plan to improve your skills, and to do so more quickly than the woman across the table is improving hers.

The legendary pros who popularized this game, players like Doyle Brunson, Johnny Moss, Nick the Greek, and others had little available to them in the way of learning materials. That's all changed. Nowadays players have their pick of how-to books, and they can supplement this by DVDs, videos, seminars, private teaching and coaching, and the Internet. There's a wealth of poker information online, from newsgroups like rec.gambling.poker to dedicated learning facilities such as Poker School Online. All of this is supplemented by a variety of online forums and blogs where players can avail themselves of information—some good, some not so good—from experts and amateurs alike. They can also post hand histories and expect to receive feedback, sometimes from very skilled professionals.

This is a wealth of information to jump-start any serious player's learning. To become a better player, there's more to learn, more to read, and you have to play, too. It takes time to convert book learning, magazine reading, and computer software savvy into real know-how. Time at the poker table is absolutely necessary to integrate knowledge into your game, so you can play efficient, effortless, consistently winning poker. To get to the finer points of the game, the basics must be second nature.

Always continue to work on your own game. Self-analytical review is the only way—outside of hiring a poker coach—to overcome bad habits and capitalize on strengths.

Learning is a never-ending process. Reading, playing, and thinking about poker—along with using the marvelous new interactive poker software available in recent years—is sufficient to give you a competence level approximating an undergraduate degree. But the real world, as any recent college graduate will attest, is always different. Poker education at an entirely new level begins in live games.

If you're really dedicated to improving your game, your quest will never end. Becoming a winning player demands continuous learning. The process of learning and thinking about poker should never cease. And you know what? The more you learn, the more you'll win, and the more enjoyment you'll derive from the game. So study up and knock 'em dead. May the flop be with you!

Index

About the Authors

The prolific LOU KRIEGER is the author of seven top-selling books on poker, including *Hold'em Excellence: From Beginner to Winner, More Hold'em Excellence: A Winner for Life, Poker for Dummies, Gambling for Dummies, Internet Poker: How to Play and Beat Online Poker Games, Winning Omaha 8 Poker,* and *The Poker Player's Bible.* He wrote a bi-weekly poker strategy column for *Card Player* magazine for more than a decade, and currently writes for *Poker Magazine.com, Poker Life* magazine, *Canadian Poker Player, Woman Poker Player* and *Midwest Gaming and Travel.* In 2000, Krieger was named one of the top one hundred gaming writers of the past one hundred years by *Casino Journal,* the industry bible. It was an honor accorded to only five poker authors. Lou Krieger has a recurring role in the poker/reality TV show, *Vegas Virgins,* the syndicated TV show *Inside Poker,* and can usually be found playing poker in the casinos and the card rooms of southern California. You can visit him online at www. loukrieger.com.

SHEREE BYKOFSKY has finished first or placed second in hundreds of poker tournaments, including taking first place out of 433 contenders in a $33 online Poker Stars tournament, winning her a seat in the 2004 World Series of Poker and a week in Vegas and cash. Sheree also won a seat in the World Championship of Online Poker. In addition to being an expert tournament poker player, Sheree is a prolific travel writer. Her articles often appear in the travel section of *Travel World*, Sogonow.com, and MSNBC.com. Sheree is the author and co-author of more than two dozen books, including *Put Your House on a Diet* (Rodale), *The Complete Idiot's Guide to Getting Published* (Alpha), and *The Poker Argument Settler* (Lyle Stuart). Sheree is a member of the Association of Author's Representatives, the American Society of Journalists and Authors, the Authors Guild and the North American Travel Journalists Association. Sheree is also an adjunct assistant professor of publishing at NYU, the 92nd Street Y, and in Cape Cod at the SEAK conferences for physicians and attorneys. Sheree's website, shereebee.com, gets an enormous amount of traffic because Sheree is also a popular literary agent who represents many authors, including several best-selling poker authors. And Sheree is proud to contribute to *Poker Life* magazine.